DISPENSATIONALISM
TODAY

DISPENSATIONALISM TODAY

By

CHARLES CALDWELL RYRIE

Foreword by
FRANK E. GAEBELEIN

MOODY PRESS

CHICAGO

ISBN: 0-8024-2256-X

Sixteenth Printing, 1980

Library of Congress Catalog Card Number: 65-14611

Printed in the United States of America

CONTENTS

FOREWORD

THE SYSTEM of Bible interpretation known as dispensationalism has in recent years been subjected to much opposition. A growing literature of books and articles has vigorously attacked it. Some have called dispensationalism a heresy and have classed it among the cults. Others have even identified it with modernism. Not all but much of the criticism of dispensationalism has come from evangelical writers.

Thus far dispensationalists have done little to answer this criticism. While they have been writing extensively, their work has not been apologetic but rather expository, particularly of the prophetic portions of Scripture. Moreover, dispensationalism has at times been the victim of some of its adherents who have pressed unwisely certain of its features.

Dr. Ryrie's book is the first book-length contemporary apologetic for dispensationalism to be written by a recognized scholar. As such it commands attention. The author, a graduate of Haverford College, Dallas Theological Seminary, and Edinburgh University (Ph.D.), is already well known for his expository and doctrinal writing. His broad experience includes service as dean of men at a Christian liberal arts college, the presidency of a leading college of Bible, and his present work as dean of the graduate school of Dallas Theological Seminary. Among his distinctions is honorary membership in Phi Beta Kappa, conferred on him by Haverford College.

Dr. Ryrie deals fairly and courteously with the critics of dispensationalism. He faces honestly objections that have been raised against this system of interpretation. He displays mastery of the literature and writes from a perspective of historical as well as contemporary theology.

7

Many who have based their condemnation of dispensationalism upon hearsay will be enlightened by Dr. Ryrie's lucid presentation of its nature and his thoughtful rebuttal of its critics. This book is an admirable contribution to better understanding among Christians who disagree about dispensationalism. Although Dr. Ryrie has deep convictions about dispensationalism and the opposition to it, he has kept his temper and presented his case candidly and graciously. The last chapter is an eloquent and reasonable plea for tolerance.

As one for whom dispensationalism is not a theology but rather a method of interpretation helpful in grasping the progress of revelation in the Bible, I do not find myself in agreement with every aspect of Dr. Ryrie's presentation. Yet I believe that his book is mandatory reading for those who have attacked dispensationalism and for all who would understand what it really is. As a reasonable and scholarly apologetic for dispensationalism it cannot be ignored.

FRANK E. GAEBELEIN

Washington, D.C.

1

DISPENSATIONALISM— HELP OR HERESY?

THE MENTION OF THE WORD *dispensationalism* usually evokes an immediate reaction. For many Christians it is a favorable reaction because they remember the help and blessing of the ministries and writings of Bible teachers who were dispensationalists. They recall the Bible conferences or special meetings or the books which awakened in them their first real interest in studying the Word seriously. For others, however, dispensationalism has upon it a question mark, for they have heard something about the teaching which has cast doubt upon its validity. Whether opposed or favorable, all admit that dispensationalism has occupied an important place in the history of the church, and that it continues to be a very live force in the life of the church today.

Like all doctrines, dispensational teaching has undergone systematization and development. In more recent times it has come under attack from a growing number of Christian leaders. Present-day dispensationalists feel strongly that their teaching is often misrepresented, and that if this were not so, many of the criticisms of dispensationalism would disappear. Therefore, this book is written for two purposes: (1) to try to correct the misconceptions about dispensationalism and thus to allay the suspicions about it and (2) to give a positive presentation of dispensationalism as it is being taught today.

It goes without saying that dispensationalists are conservative, evangelical Christians. Many of the differences of opinion which are discussed in this book are differences of some evangelicals with other evangelicals with whom there is agreement in many areas of doctrine. It is sincerely intended that what is said about these differences be written factually, fairly, and in a spirit of helpfulness. The author hopes, too, that every reader, before putting this book down, will read the last chapter, no matter how mildly or violently he may disagree with other parts of the book.

OPPOSITION TO DISPENSATIONALISM

The opposition to dispensational teaching has come from many quarters and the attacks have been quite varied in their intensity. But they all point up the need for a book of this kind, and they emphasize the need for integrity in representing the dispensational position.

The theological liberal quite naturally opposes dispensationalism, for he finds completely unpalatable its plain interpretation, which is based on a verbal, plenary view of the inspiration of Scripture. Whatever else dispensationalists are, they are conservative in their view of the fundamental doctrines of the Bible, an approach unsavory to the liberal.

But many conservatives also are opposed to the teachings of dispensationalism. On the one hand, the amillennialist recognizes that dispensationalists are invariably premillennialists, and premillennialism and amillennialism do not mix! On the other hand, those who from the viewpoint of this book may be called ultradispensationalists feel that dispensationalists have not gone far enough in their teachings and are thus unbiblical in their conclusions, which are therefore to be rejected.

Then, too, there has developed a very vocal opposition from those who want to be premillennialists without being dispensationalists. Their point is that dispensational premillennialism is not historical, but that premillennialism without dispensationalism is. Therefore their attack is centered on dispensationalism.

These various attacks range from mild to severe. Mauro, a premillennialist who abandoned the dispensational position which he once held, was bitter in his denunciation. He wrote:

> Indeed, the time is fully ripe for a thorough examination and frank exposure of this new and subtle form of *modernism* that has been spreading itself among those who have adopted the name "fundamentalists." For evangelical Christianity must purge itself of this leaven of *dispensationalism* ere it can display its former power and exert its former influence. . . . The entire system of "dispensational teaching" is *modernistic* in the strictest sense. . . .[1]

Only slightly more mild than Mauro's charge of modernism is the conclusion of Allis that dispensationalism is a "danger" and is "unscriptural."[2] More recently Daniel Fuller reached the same conclusion, namely, that dispensationalism is "internally inconsistent and unable to harmonize itself with the Biblical data. . . ."[3]

Bowman in a practically unrestrained attack on the Scofield Bible and its dispensational teachings said, "This book represents perhaps the most dangerous heresy currently to be found within Christian circles. . . ."[4] In a more temperate manner the editor of *The Presbyterian Journal,* in answer to a reader's question, called dispensationalism "a conservative 'heresy' "

[1]Philip Mauro, *The Gospel of the Kingdom* (Boston: Hamilton Brothers, 1928), pp. 8-9.
[2]Oswald T. Allis, *Prophecy and the Church* (Philadelphia: Presbyterian and Reformed Publishing Co., 1945), p. 262.
[3]Daniel Payton Fuller, "The Hermeneutics of Dispensationalism" (unpublished Doctor's dissertation, Northern Baptist Theological Seminary, Chicago, 1957), p. 386.
[4]John Wick Bowman, "The Bible and Modern Religions: II. Dispensationalism," *Interpretation,* 10 (April, 1956), 172.

since, in his own words, "whatever else you may say about a dispensationalist, one thing you can say about him with great assurance: he is conservative in theology."[5]

Of course, labeling dispensationalism as "modernism," "unscriptural," or "heresy" is not the only way it has been attacked.

Some have practiced the guilt-by-association method. Bowman, for instance, associates dispensationalism with names like Hitler and National Socialism, Roman Catholicism, Christian Science, and Mormonism.[6] The book *The Church Faces the Isms,* written by members of the faculty of the Louisville Presbyterian Theological Seminary, includes dispensationalism along with isms like Seventh-day Adventism and Perfectionism.[7]

Resort is often made to an *ad hominem* attack. The man involved is usually John Nelson Darby, and the point of attack is usually his separationist principles and practices. He is pictured as the pope of the Plymouth Brethren movement who excommunicated at will those who disagreed with him and whose separationist practices have characterized the entire dispensational movement for ill. Here is an illustration of this kind of attack:

> There exists a direct line from Darby through a number of channels . . . all characterized by and contributing to a spirit of separatism and exclusion. The devastating effects of this spirit upon the total body of Christ cannot be underestimated.[8]

Sometimes this attack takes the form of pointing to cases in which division in churches was involved in some way or another with dispensational teaching. Of course, in the report

[5]*The Presbyterian Journal,* January 2, 1963, p. 8.
[6]Bowman, *loc. cit.*
[7]Arnold B. Rhodes (ed.), *The Church Faces the Isms* (New York: Abingdon Press, 1958).
[8]Clarence B. Bass, *Backgrounds to Dispensationalism* (Grand Rapids: Wm. B. Eerdmans Publishing Co., 1960), p. 99.

of such instances the reader cannot be sure he has been given all the facts that may have contributed to the rupture. Dispensational teaching is usually made the sole cause.[9] Those who use such an argument to try to discredit the totality of dispensational teaching should call to mind some of the simple and most obvious facts about the divisive aspects of the Protestant Reformation.

There is the "intellectual" attack. The process of earning a doctor's degree has delivered the person from the dispensational teaching in which he was reared.[10] Needless to say, there are men with doctor's degrees who support the dispensational approach. However, unworthy as it may be, the attack is a powerful one. It implies that while dispensationalism is something which may inadvertently be learned in Sunday school or at a Bible school, it certainly has to be abandoned with maturity.

There is the historical attack. This will be examined later. It seeks to prove that since dispensationalism in its present form is apparently recent, it cannot be true; for surely someone would have taught it in the first eighteen centuries of the history of the church if it were true. Some who use this device to discredit dispensationalism are honest enough to admit that history is never the test of truth—the Bible and only the Bible is. But they persist in using the approach and leave the impression that history is a partly valid test, if not the final test.

There is the ridicule-of-doctrine attack. This is usually based on a straw-man construction of the dispensationalist's doctrine or on a partial statement of it. Some supposed teaching of dispensationalism is held up to ridicule and by so much the entire system is condemned. For instance, the opponents of dispensationalism are quite sure that it teaches two (or more) ways of salvation. And they ask what could be more

[9]Cf. Rhodes, *The Church Faces the Isms,* pp. 106-7.
[10]Bass, *op. cit.,* p. 9.

unscriptural than that; therefore, it is obvious that the system
is to be discarded. Or again they declare that dispensationalists will not use the Sermon on the Mount, and since the
Sermon obviously contains rich Christian truth, what could
be more apparent than that the system refusing to use it is
wrong? These charges will be discussed in due time; they are
mentioned here only as examples of the method of attack
used.

Sometimes the attack takes a very ludicrous form. For
instance, Ronald H. Nash in a recent book attempts to ridicule dispensationalism, but in the process he only shows his
own ignorance of what he is attacking. He writes:

> . . . the nondispensationalist usually finds eschatological
> factors least important. Evidently the dispensationalist
> feels that our church creeds are inadequate because they
> do not include pronouncements on such matters as a
> pretribulation rapture or the identification of the
> 144,000.[11]

Of course, the ultimate test of the truth of any doctrine is
whether it is in accord with the Biblical revelation. The
fact that the church taught something in the first century does
not make it true, and likewise if the church did not teach
something until the twentieth century, it is not necessarily
false. Tertullian, Anselm, Luther, Calvin, Darby, Scofield,
and the Westminster divines were all instruments in the
hands of God to minister truth to His church, but none of
them was perfect in all his actions. This does not make the
doctrine taught right or wrong. Defective life never enhances
doctrine, but neither does it necessarily falsify it. Too, earning a doctor's degree does not necessarily make one an expert
even in a particular field of study, and it certainly does not
make one infallible or without need of further light on a
given subject. An understanding of the truth of the Bible can

---

[11]Ronald H. Nash, *The New Evangelicalism* (Grand Rapids: Zondervan
Publishing House, 1963), p. 168.

be communicated by the Holy Spirit in and through the formal education situation and procedures, and it can be communicated apart from them.

If dispensationalism has been called everything from a "dangerous friend" to a "sworn enemy," is there any point in examining it? What do the dispensationalists say for themselves that could make their teaching even worth investigating? Could there be any help in that which is so conclusively a "heresy" in the minds of some?

THE HELP GIVEN BY DISPENSATIONALISM

A. IT ANSWERS THE NEED OF BIBLICAL DISTINCTIONS

There is no interpreter of the Bible who does not recognize the need for certain basic distinctions in the Scriptures. The theological liberal, no matter how much he speaks of the Judaistic background of Christianity, recognizes that Christianity is nevertheless different from Judaism. There may be few or many features of Judaism which in his mind carry over into Christianity, but still the message of Jesus was something new. Therefore, the material of the Old Testament is distinguished from that of the New.

The covenant theologian, for all his opposition to dispensationalism, also makes certain rather important distinctions. In fairness it must be said that his dispensational distinctions are viewed as related to the unifying and underlying covenant of grace. Nevertheless, within his concept of this covenant he does make some very basic distinctions. Berkhof will serve as an example.[12] After rejecting the usual dispensational scheme of Bible distinctions, he enumerates his own scheme of dispensations or administrations, reducing the number to two—the Old Testament dispensation and the New Testament dispensation. However, within the Old Testament dispensation Berkhof lists four subdivisions which, although he terms

---

[12]Louis Berkhof, *Systematic Theology* (Grand Rapids: Wm. B. Eerdmans Publishing Co., 1941), pp. 293-301.

them "stages in the revelation of the covenant of grace," are distinguishable enough to be listed. In reality, then, he finds these four plus the one New Testament dispensation, or five periods of differing administrations of God. Thus the covenant theologian finds Biblical distinctions a necessary part of his theology.

The dispensationalist finds his answer to the need for distinctions in his dispensational scheme. The dispensations supply the need for distinctions in the orderly progress of revelation throughout the Scriptures. His dispensations are not stages in the revelation of the covenant of grace, but are distinguishingly different administrations of God in directing the affairs of the world. It makes little difference at this point in the discussion whether there are seven dispensations or not; the point is that dispensations answer the need for distinctions.

All interpreters feel the need for distinctions. Obviously this does not prove that the dispensationalists' distinctions are the correct ones, but it demonstrates that the need for distinctions as basic to the proper interpretation of the Scriptures is recognized. There is some truth in the statements that "any person is a dispensationalist who trusts the blood of Christ rather than bringing an animal sacrifice" and "any person is a dispensationalist who observes the first day of the week rather than the seventh."[13] This is true simply because every person who does not bring an animal sacrifice or who does not observe Saturday recognizes the need for distinctions in the interpretation of the Bible. The dispensationalist feels that his system supplies the answer to that need.

B. It Answers the Need of a Philosophy of History

The Scriptures per se are not a philosophy of history, but they contain one. It is true that the Bible deals with ideas,

---

[13]L. S. Chafer, *Dispensationalism* (Dallas: Dallas Seminary Press, 1936), p. 9.

but with ideas that are interpretations of historical events. This interpretation of the meaning of historical events is the task of theology, and it is a task that is not without its problems. The chief problem is that both covenant and dispensational theology claim to represent the true philosophy of history as contained in the Scriptures. The problem is further complicated by the fact that if a philosophy of history is defined as "a systematic interpretation of universal history in accordance with a principle by which historical events and successions are unified and directed toward ultimate meaning,"[14] then in a certain sense both systems of theology meet the basic requirements of the definition. However, the way in which the two systems meet these requirements affirms that dispensationalism alone is the valid and helpful system. Notice that the definition centers in three things: (1) the recognition of "historical events and successions," or a proper concept of the progress of revelation; (2) the unifying principle; and (3) the ultimate goal of history. Let us examine both systems in relation to these three features.

Concerning the goal of history, dispensationalists find it in the establishment of the millennial kingdom on earth, while the covenant theologian regards it as the eternal state. This does not mean that dispensationalists minimize the glory of the eternal state, but they insist that the display of the glory of the God who is sovereign in human history must be seen in the present heavens and earth as well as in the new heavens and earth. This view of the realization of the goal of history within time is both optimistic and in accord with the requirements of the definition.

The covenant view, which sees the course of history continuing the present struggle between good and evil until terminated by the beginning of eternity, obviously does not have any goal within temporal history and is therefore pes-

[14]Karl Lowith, *Meaning in History* (Chicago: University of Chicago Press, 1949), p. 1.

simistic. McClain points out this contrast very clearly when he says of the covenant theology:

> According to this view, both good and evil continue in their development side by side through human history. Then will come catastrophe and the crisis of divine judgment, not for the purpose of setting up a divine kingdom in history, but after the close of history. . . . Thus history becomes the preparatory "vestibule" of eternity. . . . It is a narrow corridor, cramped and dark, a kind of "waiting room," leading nowhere *within* the historical process, but only fit to be abandoned at last for an ideal existence on another plane. Such a view of history seems unduly pessimistic, in the light of Biblical revelation.[15]

Thus, in relation to goal in a proper philosophy of history, only dispensationalism with its consummating dispensation of the millennium offers a satisfactory system.

A second requirement of a philosophy of history is a proper unifying principle. In covenant theology the principle is the covenant of grace. This is the covenant which it is alleged the Lord made with man after the Fall in which He offered salvation through Jesus Christ. In short, the covenant of grace is God's plan of salvation, and therefore the unifying principle of covenant theology is soteriological.

In dispensationalism the principle is theological or perhaps better eschatological, for the differing dispensations reveal the glory of God as He manifests His character in the differing stewardships culminating in history with the millennial glory. This is not to say that dispensationalism fails to give salvation its proper place in the purpose of God. The matter is fully discussed in chapter 6. If the goal of history is the earthly millennium, and if the glory of God will be manifest at that time in the personal presence of Christ in a way

[15]Alva J. McClain, "A Premillennial Philosophy of History," *Bibliotheca Sacra*, 113 (April, 1956), 113-14.

hitherto unknown, then the unifying principle of dispensa
tionalism may be said to be eschatological (if viewed from
the goal toward which we are moving) or theological (if
viewed from the self-revelation of God in every dispensation) .

Although the dispensationalist's principle is much broader
and therefore less confining, it must be admitted that this
alone does not prove it is the more valid one. We must also
consider the third part of our definition of a philosophy of
history.

Only dispensationalism does justice to the proper concept
of the progress of revelation. Covenant theology does include
in its system different modes of administration of the covenant
of grace, and although these modes would give an appearance
of an idea of progressiveness in revelation, in practice there
is extreme rigidity in covenant theology. James Orr, himself
a covenant theologian, criticizes the covenant system along
this very line:

> . . . it failed to seize the true idea of development, and
> by an artificial system of typology, and allegorizing in-
> terpretation, sought to read back practically the whole
> of the New Testament into the Old. But its most ob-
> vious defect was that, in using the idea of the covenant
> as an exhaustive category, and attempting to force into
> it the whole material of theology, it created an artificial
> scheme which could only repel minds desirous of simple
> and natural notions.[16]

Covenant theology, then, because of the rigidity of its unifying principle of the covenant of grace can never show within
its system proper progress of revelation.

Dispensationalism, on the other hand, can and does give
proper place to the idea of development. Under the various
administrations of God different revelation was given to man,

[16]James Orr, *The Progress of Dogma* (Grand Rapids: Wm. B. Eerdmans
Publishing Co., n.d.), p. 303.

and that revelation was increasingly progressive in the scope of its content. Though similarities are present in various dispensations, they are part of a true development and not a result of employing the unifying principle of the covenant of grace. The particular manifestations of the will of God in each dispensation are given their full yet distinctive place in the progress of the revelation of God throughout the ages. Only dispensationalism can cause historical events and successions to be seen in their own light and not to be reflected in the artificial light of an overall covenant.

Thus a correct philosophy of history with its requirements of a proper goal, a proper unifying principle, and a proper concept of progress is best satisfied by the dispensational system. Like the approach of Biblical distinctions, the approach through the proper concept of the philosophy of history leads to dispensationalism.

C. It Provides Consistent Hermeneutics

To this subject a chapter will be devoted later in the book. Suffice it to say at this point that dispensationalism claims to employ principles of literal, plain or normal, interpretation consistently.

Covenant theologians are well known for their stand on allegorical interpretation especially as it relates to the prophetic Word, and they are equally well known for their amillennialism which is only the natural outcome of allegorizing. Premillennialists who are not dispensationalists also have to depart from normal interpretation at certain points in their eschatology. For example, Ladd, in order to add support to his posttribulational view, is forced to regard the 144,000 of Revelation 7 as referring not to literal Israel but to spiritual Israel or the Church.[17] Further, he cannot agree with the

[17]George E. Ladd, *The Blessed Hope* (Grand Rapids: Wm. B. Eerdmans Publishing Co., 1956), p. 126.

dispensationalists' idea of the Jewish character of Matthew's Gospel,[18] but he nowhere explains, for instance, how he can interpret in any normal way our Lord's words of commission to the Twelve recorded in Matthew 10:5-10. Anyone who attempts to interpret plainly this commission which forbade the disciples to go to the Gentiles, and the commission which commands the same group to go to the Gentiles (Matt. 28: 19-20) either gives up in confusion or resorts to spiritualizing one of the passages or recognizes a dispensational distinction. If plain or normal interpretation is the only valid hermeneutical principle, and if it is consistently applied, it will cause one to be a dispensationalist. As basic as one believes normal interpretation to be, to that extent he will of necessity become a dispensationalist.

Dispensationalism, then, claims to be a help in supplying the answer to the need for Biblical distinction, in offering a satisfying philosophy of history, and in employing a consistently normal principle of interpretation. These are basic areas in proper understanding of the Bible. If dispensationalism has the answers, then it is the most helpful tool in Biblical interpretation. If not, it ought to be discarded as worthless.

[18]*Ibid.*, pp. 133-34.

2

WHAT IS A DISPENSATION?

THERE IS NO MORE PRIMARY PROBLEM in the whole matter of dispensationalism than that of definition. By this is meant not simply arriving at a single sentence definition of the word, but rather a complete definition and description of the concept. This will require an examination of the Scriptural use of the word, a comparison of the word *dispensation* with related words such as *age*, a study of the use of the word in church history, and some observations concerning the characteristics and number of the dispensations.

To say that there is a great lack of clear thinking on this matter of definition is an understatement. Both dispensationalists and nondispensationalists are guilty of lack of clarity. Most from both groups are quite satisfied to use the well-known definition that appears in the notes of the Scofield Reference Bible: "A dispensation is a period of time during which man is tested in respect of obedience to some *specific* revelation of the will of God. Seven such dispensations are distinguished in Scripture."[1] Dispensationalists use this definition without thinking further of its implications in relation to *age*, for instance, and without ever examining its basis or lack of basis in the Scriptural revelation itself. Nondispensationalists use it as a convenient and useful scapegoat simply because it does not (and could not in two sentences)

[1]The Scofield Reference Bible (New York: Oxford University Press, 1945), p. 5.

22

convey all that is involved in the concept of a dispensation. If this concise definition were all that Scofield had to say about dispensations, then it would be fair to concentrate an attack on it, but if he has more to say (which he does) then it is hardly fair.

For instance—to draw an analogy in another doctrinal area, a conservative when pressed for a concise statement of his theory of the atonement will answer, "I believe in substitutionary atonement." This is entirely accurate and probably the best concise answer that could be given. But liberals are well-known for using this simple statement as a means of ridicule, for they point out that the work of Christ cannot be confined to a single aspect like substitution. This is true, and the conservative recognizes that the entire work of Christ cannot be fully expressed by the single word *substitution.* Nevertheless, all the work of Christ is based on His vicarious sacrifice.

In like manner, the nondispensationalist points out some lack in Scofield's definition and with a wave of the hand dismisses dispensationalism on the basis of the weakness of the definition! Perhaps Scofield's definition does not distinguish dispensation from age, but such failure does not mean that they cannot be distinguished or that they have not been by others. And it certainly does not mean that the entire system is condemned. Bowman resorts to this stratagem when he declares: ". . . the word translated 'dispensation' in the Greek Bible . . . never means nor does it ever have any reference to a period of time as such, as Scofield's definition demands."[2] Though the accuracy of Bowman's statement may be questioned by the references in Ephesians 1:10 and 3:9, in making such a charge against Scofield's definition Bowman attempts to discredit the entire system.

The popularity of the Scofield Reference Bible has focused

[2]John Wick Bowman, "The Bible and Modern Religions: II. Dispensationalism," *Interpretation,* 10 (April, 1956), 174.

considerable attention on the definition in its notes and has made it the prime target for attack by nondispensationalists. However, scholars who are critical of dispensationalism should recognize that Scofield is not the only one who has defined the word, and if there are weaknesses in his definition, they ought to recognize that others may have offered definitions which eliminate the weaknesses. At any rate, any scholarly critique should certainly take into account several definitions if the system is to be represented fairly. For instance, Chafer did not emphasize the time aspect in a dispensation in his concept,[3] and more recently the present writer defined a dispensation entirely in terms of economy rather than age.[4] Any critique ought to take into account such definitions as well as Scofield's.

ETYMOLOGY OF THE WORD DISPENSATION

The English word *dispensation* is an anglicized form of the Latin *dispensatio* which the Vulgate uses to translate the Greek word. The Latin verb is a compound, meaning "to weigh out or dispense."[5] There are three principal ideas connected with the meaning of the English word: (1) "The action of dealing out or distributing"; (2) "the action of administering, ordering, or managing; the system by which things are administered"; and (3) "the action of dispensing with some requirement."[6] In further defining the use of the word theologically, the same dictionary says that a dispensation is "a stage in a progressive revelation, expressly adapted to the needs of a particular nation or period of time . . . also, the age or period during which a system has prevailed."[7] It

---

[3]L. S. Chafer, *Dispensationalism* (Dallas: Seminary Press, 1936), pp. 8-9.
[4]Charles C. Ryrie, "The Necessity of Dispensationalism," *Bibliotheca Sacra*, 114 (July, 1957), 251.
[5]W. W. Skeat, *An Etymological Dictionary of the English Language* (Oxford: Clarendon Press, 1946), p. 174.
[6]*The Oxford English Dictionary* (Oxford University Press, 1933), III, 481.
[7]*Ibid.*

is interesting to notice, in view of the usual criticism of Scofield's definition, that in this dictionary definition *dispensation* and *age* are very closely related.

The Greek word *oikonomia* comes from the verb which means to manage, regulate, administer, and plan.[8] The word itself is a compound whose parts mean literally "to divide, apportion, administer or manage the affairs of an inhabited house." In the papyri the officer (*oikonomos*) who administered a dispensation was referred to as a steward or managei of an estate, or as a treasurer.[9] Thus the central idea in the word *dispensation* is that of managing or administering the affairs of a household.

SCRIPTURAL USE OF THE WORD DISPENSATION

A. The Usage of the Word

The various forms of the word *dispensation* are used in the New Testament twenty times. The verb *oikonomeo* is used once in Luke 16:2 where it is translated "to be a steward." The noun *oikonomos* is used ten times (Luke 12:42; 16:1, 3, 8; Rom. 16:23; I Cor. 4:1, 2; Gal. 4:2; Titus 1:7; I Pet. 4:10), and in all instances it is translated "steward" except "chamberlain" in Romans 16:23. The noun *oikonomia* is used nine times (Luke 16:2, 3, 4; I Cor. 9:17; Eph. 1:10; 3:2, 9; Col. 1:25; I Tim. 1:4). In these instances it is translated variously ("stewardship," "dispensation," "edifying"). The Authorized Version of Ephesians 3:9 has "fellowship" (*koinonia*), whereas the American Standard Version has "dispensation."

B. The Features Displayed

Before attempting any formal definition, it might be useful to note some of the features connected with the word itself as

---

[8]W. F. Arndt and F. W. Gingrich, *A Greek-English Lexicon of the New Testament* (Chicago: University of Chicago Press, 1957), p. 562.

[9]J. H. Moulton and George Milligan, *The Vocabulary of the Greek Testament* (Grand Rapids: Wm. B. Eerdmans Publishing Co., 1949), pp. 442-43.

it appears in the New Testament. These are not necessarily features of the dispensational scheme but are simply observable connections in which the word is used. In Christ's teaching the word is confined to two parables recorded in Luke (12:42; 16:1, 3, 8). In both cases the parables concern the management of a household by a steward, but the parable recorded in Luke 16 gives some important characteristics of a stewardship or dispensational arrangement. These characteristics include the following:

(1) Basically there are two parties—the one whose authority it is to delegate duties and the one whose responsibility it is to carry out these charges. The rich man and the steward play these roles in the parable of Luke 16 (v. 1).

(2) There are specific responsibilities. In the parable the steward failed in his known duties when he wasted the goods of his lord (v. 1).

(3) Accountability as well as responsibility is part of the arrangement. A steward may be called to account for the discharge of his stewardship at any time, for it is the lord's prerogative to expect faithful obedience to the duties entrusted to the steward (v. 2).

(4) A change may be made at any time unfaithfulness is found in the existing administration. ("Mayest be no longer steward" is better translated "cannot longer be steward.")

These four features give some idea of what was involved in the concept of a dispensational arrangement as the word was used in the time of Christ.

The other occurrences of the words are all in the writings of Paul except for the reference in I Peter 4:10. Certain features of the concept are evident from these usages.

(1) God is the one to whom men are responsible in the discharge of their stewardship obligations. In three instances this relationship to God is mentioned by Paul (I Cor. 4:1-2; Titus 1:7).

(2) Faithfulness is required of those to whom a dispensational responsibility is committed (I Cor. 4:2). This is illustrated by Erastus, who held the important position of treasurer (steward) of the city (Rom. 16:23).

(3) A stewardship may end at an appointed time (Gal. 4:2). In this reference the end of the stewardship came because of a different purpose being introduced. This reference also shows that a dispensation is connected with time.

(4) Dispensations are connected with the mysteries of God, i.e., with specific revelation from God (I Cor. 4:1; Eph. 3:2; Col. 1:25).

(5) Dispensation and age are connected ideas, but the words are not exactly interchangeable. For instance, Paul declares that the revelation of the present dispensation was hidden "for ages" (Eph. 3:9). The same thing is said in Colossians 1:26. However, since a dispensation operates within a time period, the concepts have some interrelation.

(6) At least three dispensations (as commonly understood in dispensational teaching) are mentioned by Paul. In Ephesians 1:10 he writes of "the dispensation of the fullness of times," which seems to be a future period. In Ephesians 3:2 he designates the "dispensation of the grace of God," which was the emphasis of the content of his preaching at that time. In Colossians 1:25-26 it is implied that another dispensation preceded the present one in which the mystery of Christ in the believer is revealed.

It is very important to notice that in the first two of these instances *there can be no question that the Bible uses the word dispensation in exactly the same way the dispensationalist does.* Even Bowman admits: "Actually, of all seven dispensations accepted by Scofield and his colleagues, there are but two (Grace and the Fullness of Time) in connection with which the word 'dispensation' is ever used at all."[10]

[10]Bowman, *op. cit.*, p. 175.

The negative cast of Bowman's statement must not obscure the importance of this point. The Bible does name two dispensations in the same way that dispensationalists do (and implies a third). Granted, it does not name seven, but since it does name two, perhaps there is something to this teaching called dispensationalism.

Almost all opponents of dispensationalism try to make much of their claim that the Scriptures do not use the word dispensation in the same theological and technical sense that the dispensational scheme of teaching does. Two facts should be pointed out in answer to this charge. The first has already been stated in the preceding paragraph: the Scripture on at least two occasions does use the word in the same way the dispensationalist does. Thus the charge is simply not true.

Second, it should be remembered that it is perfectly valid to take a Biblical word and use it in a theological sense *as long as the theological use is not unbiblical.* This all conservatives do with the word *atonement.* It is a word that is never used in the New Testament, yet theologically all use it to stand for what is involved in the death of Christ. Biblically the word *atonement* is not used in connection with the death of Christ, but since it is used of the covering for sin in the Old Testament, it is not unbiblical to give it a theological meaning that is in reality more inclusive than its strict Biblical usage. The dispensationalist does a similar thing with the word *dispensation.* The usage of the word and the features of the word as outlined above prove conclusively that the dispensationalist has in no way used the word in an unbiblical sense when he uses it as a designation for his system of teaching. Even Fuller admits this: "It is this latter sense which gives rise to the perfectly valid theological usage of the word 'dispensation' to denote a period of time during which God deals with man in a certain way."[11]

[11]Daniel P. Fuller, "The Hermeneutics of Dispensationalism" (Doctor's dissertation, Northern Baptist Theological Seminary, Chicago, 1957), p. 20.

To summarize: Dispensationalism views the world as a household run by God. In this household-world God is dispensing or administering its affairs according to His own will and in various stages of revelation in the process of time. These various stages mark off the distinguishably different economies in the outworking of His total purpose, and these economies are the dispensations. The understanding of God's differing economies is essential to a proper interpretation of His revelation within those various economies.

Before leaving the subject of definition, it may be helpful to append several other useful definitions of a dispensation. Scroggie, a noted Scottish writer and pastor, defined it this way:

> The word *oikonomia* bears one significance, and means "an administration," whether of a house, or property, of a state, or a nation, or as in the present study, *the administration of the human race or any part of it,* at any given time. Just as a parent would govern his household in different ways, according to varying necessity, yet ever for one good end, so God has at different times dealt with men in different ways, according to the necessity of the case, but throughout for one great, grand end.[14]

Ironside, prince of dispensational preachers, defined it this way:

> An economy is an ordered condition of things. . . . There are various economies running through the Word of God. A dispensation, an economy, then, is that particular order or condition of things prevailing in one special age which does not necessarily prevail in another.[15]

Clarence E. Mason, Jr., dean of Philadelphia College of Bible, includes descriptive features of dispensations in his definition:

[14]W. Graham Scroggie, *Ruling Lines of Progressive Revelation* (London: Morgan and Scott, 1918), pp. 62-63.
[15]H. A. Ironside, *In the Heavenlies* (New York: Loizeaux Brothers, n.d.), p. 67.

The word *dispensation* means literally a *stewardship* or *administration* or *economy*. Therefore, in its Biblical usage, a *dispensation* is a divinely established steward-ship of a particular revelation of God's mind and will which brings added responsibility to the whole race of men or that portion of the race to whom the revelation is particularly given by God.

Associated with the revelation, on the one hand, are promises of reward or blessing for those responding to the obedience of faith, while on the other hand there are warnings of judgment upon those who do not respond in the obedience of faith to that particular revelation.

However, though the time period *(age)* ends, certain principles of the revelation *(dispensation* or steward-ship) are often carried over into succeeding ages, be-cause God's truth does not cease to be truth, and these principles become part of the cumulative body of truth for which man is responsible in the progressive unfold-ing revelation of God's redemptive purpose.[16]

Another definition also includes descriptive elements:

A dispensation is God's distinctive method of governing mankind or a group of men during a period of human history, marked by a crucial event, test, failure, and judgment. From the divine standpoint, it is a steward-ship, a rule of life, or a responsibility for managing God's affairs in His house. From the historical stand-point, it is a stage in the progress of revelation.[17]

The differentiation of viewpoints in this definition is a very helpful distinction. A dispensation is from God's view-point an economy; from man's, a responsibility; and in rela-tion to progressive revelation, a stage in it. The connection

[16]C. E. Mason, Jr., "Eschatology" (mimeographed notes for course at Philadelphia College of Bible, rev. 1962), pp. 5-6.
[17]Paul David Nevin, "Some Major Problems in Dispensational Interpre-tation" (unpublished Doctor's dissertation, Dallas Theological Seminary, 1963), p. 97.

between dispensationalism and progressive revelation deserves further elaboration.

THE RELATION OF THE DISPENSATIONS TO PROGRESSIVE REVELATION

Progressive revelation is the recognition that God's message to man was not given in one single act but was unfolded in a long series of successive acts and through the minds and hands of many men of varying backgrounds. It is, so to speak, a theistic view of revelation rather than a deistic view. The pages of the Bible present "not the exposition of a revelation completed, but the records of a revelation in progress. Its parts and features are seen, not as arranged after their development, but as arranging themselves in the course of their development, and growing, through stages which can be marked, and by accessions which can be measured, into the perfect form which they attain at last."[18]

The principle of progressive revelation is evident in the Scriptures themselves. Paul told his audience on Mars Hill that in a former day God overlooked their ignorance, but now He commands repentance (Acts 17:30). The majestic opening of the book of Hebrews emphatically outlines the various means of progressive revelation (Heb. 1:1-2). One of the most striking verses that shows the different ways of God's dealing with mankind is John 1:17: "For the law was given by Moses, but grace and truth came by Jesus Christ." God's truth was obviously not given all at one time, and the varying stages of revelation show that He has worked in different ways at different times. The Bible interpreter must observe carefully this progressiveness of revelation, and dispensationalism helps promote accuracy in this regard.

In this matter of the correct observation and interpretation of the progress of revelation we see the close connection be-

[18]T. D. Bernard, *The Progress of Doctrine in the New Testament* (Grand Rapids: Zondervan Publishing House, n.d.), p. 20.

tween dispensationalism and hermeneutics. A standard text on hermeneutics, which first appeared in 1883 and which has no dispensational ax to grind, says: "With each new series of generations some new promise is given, or some great purpose of God is brought to light."[19] It is the marking off of these stages in the revelation of the purpose of God that is the basis for the dispensational approach to the interpretation of the Scriptures. Even Ramm, who is not now a dispensationalist, admits that a clearer realization of progressive revelation has been largely due to the "beneficial influence of dispensationalism."[20]

Nondispensational interpreters (of the covenant theology school) have been guilty of reading back (and sometimes forcing back) the teaching of the New Testament into the Old especially in order to try to substantiate their doctrine of salvation in the Old Testament. Dispensationalists, on the other hand, have been guilty of making such hard and fast distinctions between the ages involved in the various dispensations that they, for instance, have said very little about grace in the Old Testament. However, though both groups are blameworthy, the covenant theologian's faulty interpretation is a result of a basically inherent defect in his system, while the dispensationalist's lack is not in the system but in the expounding of it. Covenant theology allows for and even demands this reading back of the New Testament into the Old. Dispensational theology, while recognizing definite and distinguishable distinctions, asserts the basic unity of the unfolding plan of God in the Scriptures.

Nevertheless, dispensationalists have not always asserted this unity as they might have, and therefore it has become a common thing to indict dispensationalism on this matter. "Dispensationalism destroys the unity of the Bible" is the cry. Be-

[19]Milton S. Terry, *Biblical Hermeneutics* (Grand Rapids: Zondervan Publishing House, n.d.), p. 568.
[20]Bernard Ramm, *Protestant Biblical Interpretation* (rev. ed.; Boston: W. A. Wilde, 1956), p. 158.

cause of the dispensational scheme, one writer declares, "the Bible ceases to be a self-consistent whole."[21] "This theory," charges Berkhof, "is also divisive in tendency, dismembering the organism of Scripture with disastrous results."[22]

More popularly this objection is expressed by the charge that dispensationalists see no value in the Sermon on the Mount, or that they will not pray the Lord's prayer.[23]

Even though dispensationalists may not have clearly communicated the teachings of their system along these lines, it must be remembered that the system is not at fault. Dispensationalism alone has a broad enough unifying principle to do justice to the unity of the progress of revelation on the one hand and the distinctiveness of the various stages in that progress on the other. Covenant theology can only emphasize the unity, and in so doing overemphasizes it until it becomes the sole governing category of interpretation. In covenant theology this is the chief principle of interpretation. Any seeming disunity in the dispensational scheme is superficial, and in reality one feels that the much publicized supposed conflicts of dispensationalism exist in the minds of the covenant theologians and are aggravated by their own unwarranted unified approach to the Scriptures. *Variety can be an essential part of unity.* This is true of God's creation; it is also true of God's revelation; and only dispensationalism can adequately account for the variety of distinguishable economies or dispensations *in* (not apart from) the outworking of God's purpose.

To summarize: Progressive revelation views the Bible not as a textbook on theology but as the continually unfolding

---

[21]Oswald T. Allis, "Modern Dispensationalism and the Law of God," *The Evangelical Quarterly*, 8 (July 15, 1936), 272.

[22]Louis Berkhof, *Systematic Theology* (Grand Rapids: Wm. B. Eerdmans Publishing Co., 1941), p. 291.

[23]For example, T. A. Hegre, *The Cross and Sanctification* (Minneapolis: Bethany Fellowship, 1960), p. 6. Cf. the entire chapter entitled "Have You Lost Your Bible?" which devotes two pages to the disastrous effects of liberalism on the Bible and five pages to the "damaging" results of dispensationalism!

revelation of God given by various means throughout the successive ages. In this unfolding there are distinguishable stages of revelation when God introduces new things for which man becomes responsible. These stages are the economies, stewardships, or dispensations in the unfolding of His purpose. Dispensationalism, therefore, recognizes both the unity of His purpose and the diversity in the unfolding of it. Covenant theology emphasizes the unity only to the point of forcing unwarranted, inconsistent, and contradictory interpretation of the Scriptures. Only dispensationalism can maintain the unity and diversity at the same time and offer a consistent, cohesive, and complementary system of interpretation.

CHARACTERISTICS OF A DISPENSATION

A. PRIMARY CHARACTERISTICS

What marks off the various economies in the outworking of God's purpose and distinguishes each from the other? The answer is twofold: (1) the different governing relationship into which God enters with the world in each economy and (2) the resulting responsibility on mankind in each of these different relationships.

These characteristics are vitally bound up with the different revelations God gave throughout history and show again the link between each dispensation and the various stages in the progress of revelation. Without meaning at all to prejudge the question of how many dispensations there are, let us see if this answer is valid, using several unquestioned dispensations as illustrations.

Before sin entered at the Fall of man, God's governmental relationship with Adam and Eve was direct. Their responsibility was to maintain that direct fellowship with Him, and this involved specifically dressing the garden and abstaining from eating the fruit of the tree of the knowledge of good and evil. After sin entered at the Fall, God's relationship was no longer always direct, for a barrier had come between Him and man.

At the giving of the law to the Israelites through Moses God's government was mediated through the various categories of the law. This does not mean that He never spoke directly, but it does mean that His principal mode of government was the Mosaic code, which was a new thing introduced at that time. It also means that the responsibility upon mankind was conformity to that code—again a new responsibility, for prior to the giving of the law man was obviously not held responsible for something that did not exist.

After the coming of Christ, God's governing relationship with mankind was no longer through the Mosaic law. The rent veil and the end of approach to God through the sacrificial system show this. Witness, too, the distinguishable difference in relation to justification as summarized by Paul in his sermon at Antioch in Pisidia: "And by him all that believe are justified from all things, from which ye could not be justified by the law of Moses" (Acts 13:39). Here is unquestionably a distinguishably different way of running the affairs of the world in regard to man's responsibility in relation to the most important area of justification. Whatever his responsibility was under the Mosaic law may be left unspecified at present (see chapter 6), but with the coming of Christ the requirement for justification became faith in Him. This, too, is obviously a distinctive stage in the progress of revelation. Therefore, we conclude that a new dispensation was inaugurated, since the economy and responsibility changed and new revelation was given.

Thus the distinguishing characteristics of a different dispensation are: (1) a change in God's governmental relationship with man (though a dispensation does not have to be composed entirely of completely new features), (2) a resultant change in man's responsibility, and (3) corresponding revelation necessary to effect the change (which new revelation is a stage in the progress of revelation through the Bible).

B. SECONDARY CHARACTERISTICS

Thus far nothing has been said about the usual characteristics listed for a new dispensation: namely, a test, a failure, and a judgment. The test is practically the same as the human responsibility. Obviously, whenever God gives revelation concerning His method of running the affairs of the world, there is also given a corresponding responsibility or test to man as to whether or not he will align himself with God's economy and the revelation of it. Opponents of dispensationalism, who insist that such testing on God's part makes Him little more than an experimenter apparently not knowing how things will turn out, in reality fail to understand the purpose of testing in general.[24] After all, a dispensational test is no different essentially from the tests spoken of by James in chapter 1 of his epistle. Such tests are not for the purpose of enlightening God but for the purpose of bringing out what is in man, whether faith or failure.

In one sense every dispensation contains the same test: Will man respond favorably toward the responsibility of the particular economy under which he is living? Specifically, this general test is particularized in each dispensation by the nature of the revelation God gave in each instance concerning man's responsibility. Actually, every part of the revelation belonging to each dispensation is a part of the test, and the totality of the revelation is the test. Dispensationalists have often in their writings tried to isolate the particular test of each dispensation and, while this may be helpful to the student, it can only be at best a partial statement of the entire responsibility.[25]

[24]Bowman, *op. cit.*, p. 176.
[25]C. I. Scofield, *Rightly Dividing the Word of Truth* (New York: Fleming H. Revell Co., n.d.).

Is failure a necessary part of each dispensation? It is a fact of Biblical history that man has failed throughout all the ages of time. Each dispensation is filled with failures simply because history is. The failures are in at least two realms—the realm of governmental economy and the realm of salvation. In both areas not all men have failed, but in both realms most men have. Sin often seems to come to a climax at certain points in human history, and such climaxes mark the end of the various dispensations. The crucifixion of Christ was the climax of rebellion of the nation that had been given the privilege of the law and the service of God. It also marked the end of a dispensation. The present age will be climaxed by rebellion and a turning away from God in force. The millennial kingdom will be climaxed by widespread rebellion against the personal reign of Christ the King (Rev. 20:7-9).

Does each dispensation have a judgment? Actually each may have many judgments, just as it may have many testings and failures. But if there is a climactic failure, then there is also a climactic judgment. While the matters of testing, failure, and judgment are not the basics that mark off the dispensations, they seem to be part and parcel of them. If, however, there were no decisive test there still could be a dispensational arrangement. If there were no climactic failure and judgment, there still could be a change in the dispensational arrangement. The presence of a test, failure, and judgment is not the *sine qua non* of a dispensational government of the world.

C. OBJECTIONS

Do not these characteristics seem to dissect history and compartmentalize its eras? From one viewpoint dispensationalism does appear to do so. This cross-sectional perspective of the dispensational scheme is the view usually presented in dispensational charts. While *there is nothing erroneous about it,* it is not the whole story. There is also what may be called the longitudinal perspective in dispensationalism.[26] This includes the continuing principles through all dispensations which give coherency to the whole course of history. The distinctive governmental arrangement that distinguishes the various dispensations in no way conflicts with the unities of Scripture.

The longitudinal perspective, for example, emphasizes the fact that God is, has been, and will be, a God of grace. The cross-sectional perspective emphasizes the government of grace which prevails today. The longitudinal perspective is that of the progress of revelation; the cross-sectional is that at any given point of time. Both perspectives are not only valid but necessary in understanding God's revelation.

Thus it is a ridiculous objection to say, "If . . . God is always gracious, then it is confusing to distinguish a particular age by a term that characterizes all ages."[27] One might ask if God has not always been a God of law? And if so, is it wrong to delineate a period called the Law? Does not God Himself through John make these distinctions (John 1:17)? The objection is based on a false premise which Fuller reveals in this further statement: "Hence it is impossible to think of varying degrees of grace, for God either is or is not gracious."[28] The fact of the matter simply is that there are varying degrees of the *revelation* of God's grace, even though when there is less revelation, God is not less gracious than when there is greater revelation of His grace. If the theology of Fuller's statement were sound, then God could be construed not to be very holy and righteous and just whenever He delays or defers immediate and justifiable judgment. He simply reveals His wrath more specifically at certain times in human history

---

[26]H. Chester Woodring, "Grace Under the Mosaic Covenant" (unpublished Doctor's dissertation, Dallas Theological Seminary, 1956), pp. 33-38.
[27]Fuller, *op. cit.*, p. 164.
[28]*Ibid.*

than at others. But periods of silence do not make Him less righteous any more than a veiled revelation of grace makes Him less gracious. Only dispensationalism with its cross-sectional and longitudinal perspectives can recognize the wealth, mobility, and complexity of the history of God's running the affairs of this world.

Before either the covenant or dispensational systems had been developed, Calvin wrote these appropriate words:

> It is not fitting, they say, that God, always self-consistent, should permit such a great change, disapproving afterward what he had once commanded and commended. I reply that God ought not to be considered changeable merely because he accommodated diverse forms to different ages, as he knew would be expedient for each. If a farmer sets certain tasks for his household in the winter, other tasks for the summer, we shall not on this account accuse him of inconstancy, or think that he departs from the proper rule of agriculture, which accords with the continuous order of nature. In like manner, if a householder instructs, rules, and guides his children one way in infancy, another way in youth, and still another in young manhood, we shall not on this account call him fickle and say that he abandons his purpose. Why, then, do we brand God with the mark of inconstancy because he has with apt and fitting marks distinguished a diversity of times?[29]

Covenant theology with its all-encompassing covenant of grace glosses over great epochs and climaxes of history lest they disturb the "unity of Scripture" and introduce something so new that a dispensation might have to be recognized. Especially is this true in connection with the Church as a new thing. The cross-sectional view emphasizes the distinctive importance of each event in its historical setting and for its particular purpose; the longitudinal view places all events in

[29]John Calvin, *Institutes of the Christian Religion*, II, XI, 13.

their proper relationship in the total progress of revelation. Dispensationalism avoids confusion and contradiction and at the same time unites all the parts into the whole.

The once-for-all yet progressive character of dispensational distinctions prohibits that they should be intermingled or confused as they are chronologically successive. But it has been charged these characteristics of test, failure and judgment form a repeated cyclical pattern of history like that of the pagan Greeks. Thus Kraus says: "The philosophy of history is essentially the Greek concept of cycles, each cycle ending in apostasy and judgment. God is not represented as working out His plan *in the historical process,* but as appearing intermittently, as it were, to begin a new cycle by supernatural intervention."[30] Chapter 1 points out that only dispensationalism presents a properly optimistic philosophy of history. Furthermore, the charts notwithstanding, the dispensational pattern does not form a repetitive cyclical picture, but rather an ascending spiral. Sauer, whose books combine so ably both the cross-sectional and the longitudinal perspectives of dispensationalism, summarizes the matter in this way:

> But a fresh Divine beginning is never merely a return to the old. In each reformation born out of collapse lay at the same time the seed of a life-program for the future. Revelation and development are in no case opposites but belong together. In the sphere of the Bible, as elsewhere, there is an ascent from lower to higher, from twilight to clearness . . .[31]

This spiral concept is readily seen by imagining the confusion of inverting the dispensational order and placing the millennium first. Just as illogical would be the reversing of law and grace (or whatever names you wish to attach to that which came through Moses and that which was revealed

[30]C. Norman Kraus, *Dispensationalism in America* (Richmond: John Knox Press, 1958), p. 126.
[31]Sauer, *op. cit.,* p. 54.

through Christ) . Dispensationalism reveals the outworking
of God's plan in the historical process in a progressive revelation of His glory. It magnifies the grace of God, for it recognizes that true progress can come only from God's gracious
intervention in human society. If there were not "cyclical"
interventions, then the course of history would be only down-
ward and entirely pessimistic.

To summarize: The principal characteristic of a dispensation is the economic arrangement and responsibility which
God reveals in each dispensation. Such responsibility is a test
in itself. Most men fail the test, and then judgment follows.
The dispensational scheme has two perspectives—a cross-sectional aspect (which is sometimes misconstrued as cycles but
which is in reality a spiral) and a longitudinal aspect (which
emphasizes the unfolding progress of revelation and continuing principles throughout the ages of the dispensations) .

THE *SINE QUA NON* OF DISPENSATIONALISM

What marks off a man as a dispensationalist? What is the
sine qua non of the system? Even though certain later discussions must be anticipated in order to answer the question,
it seems appropriate to give an answer at this point.

Theoretically the *sine qua non* ought to lie in the recognition of the fact that God has distinguishably different economies in governing the affairs of the world. Covenant theologians hold that there are various dispensations (and even use
the word!) within the outworking of the covenant of grace.
Hodge, for instance, believed that there are four dispensations
after the Fall—Adam to Abraham, Abraham to Moses, Moses
to Christ, and Christ to the end.[32] Louis Berkhof writes, as we
have seen, of only two basic dispensations—the Old and the
New, but within the Old he sees four periods and all of these

[32]Charles Hodge, *Systematic Theology* (Grand Rapids: Wm. B. Eerdmans
Publishing Co., 1946), II, 373-77.

are revelations of the covenant of grace.[33] In other words, a man can believe in dispensations, and even see them in relation to progressive revelation, without being a dispensationalist.

Is the essence of dispensationalism in the number of dispensations? No, for this is in no way a major issue in the system, as will be discussed in the next chapter. It is not the fact that Scofield taught seven dispensations and Hodge only four that makes the former a dispensationalist and the latter not.

Perhaps the issue of premillennialism is determinative. Again the answer is negative, for there are those who are premillennial who definitely are not dispensational. The covenant premillennialist holds to the concept of the covenant of grace and the central soteriological purpose of God. He retains the idea of the millennial kingdom, though he finds little support for it in the Old Testament prophecies since he generally assigns them to the Church. The kingdom in his view is markedly different from that which is taught by dispensationalists since it loses much of its Jewish character due to the slighting of the Old Testament promises concerning the kingdom. Many covenant premillennialists are also post-tribulationalists, and this is doubtless a logical accompaniment of the nondispensational approach.[34] At any rate, being a premillennialist does not necessarily make one a dispensationalist. (However, the reverse is true—being a dispensationalist makes one a premillennialist.)

What, then, is the *sine qua non* of dispensationalism? The answer is threefold.

(1) A dispensationalist keeps Israel and the Church distinct. This is stated in different ways by both friends and foes of dispensationalism. Fuller says that "the basic premise

[33]Berkhof, *op. cit.*, pp. 293-300.
[34]H. Phillip Hook, "The Doctrine of the Kingdom in Covenant Premillennialism" (unpublished Doctor's dissertation, Dallas Theological Seminary, 1959). Cf. Fuller, *op. cit.*, pp. 363-64.

of Dispensationalism is two purposes of God expressed in the formation of two peoples who maintain their distinction throughout eternity."[35] Gaebelein stated it in terms of the difference between the Jews, the Gentiles and the Church of God.[36] Chafer summarized it as follows:

> The dispensationalist believes that throughout the ages God is pursuing two distinct purposes: one related to the earth with earthly people and earthly objectives involved which is Judaism; while the other is related to heaven with heavenly people and heavenly objectives involved, which is Christianity. . . . Over against this, the partial dispensationalist, though dimly observing a few obvious distinctions, bases his interpretation on the supposition that God is doing but one thing, namely, the general separation of the good from the bad, and, in spite of all the confusion this limited theory creates, contends that the earthly people merge into the heavenly people; that the earthly program must be given a spiritual interpretation or disregarded altogether.[37]

This is probably the most basic theological test of whether or not a man is a dispensationalist, and it is undoubtedly the most practical and conclusive. A man who fails to distinguish Israel and the Church will inevitably not hold to dispensational distinctions; and one who does, will.

(2) This distinction between Israel and the Church is born out of a system of hermeneutics which is usually called literal interpretation. Therefore, the second aspect of the *sine qua non* of dispensationalism is the matter of plain hermeneutics. The word *literal* is perhaps not so good as either the word *normal* or *plain,* but in any case it is interpretation that does not spiritualize or allegorize as nondispensational interpretation does. The spiritualizing may be

[35]Fuller, *op. cit.,* p. 25.
[36]Arno C. Gaebelein, *The Gospel of Matthew* (New York: *Our Hope,* 1910), I, 4.
[37]Chafer, *op. cit.,* p. 107.

practiced to a lesser or greater degree, but its presence in a system of interpretation is indicative of a nondispensational approach.[38] Consistently literal or plain interpretation is indicative of a dispensational approach to the interpretation of the Scriptures. And it is this very consistency—the strength of dispensational interpretation—that irks the nondispensationalist and becomes the object of his ridicule.[39]

(3) A third aspect of the *sine qua non* of dispensationalism is a rather technical matter which will be discussed more fully later (chapter 5). It concerns the underlying purpose of God in the world. The covenant theologian in practice makes this purpose salvation, and the dispensationalist says the purpose is broader than that, namely, the glory of God. To the dispensationalist the soteriological or saving program of God is not the only program but one of the means God is using in the total program of glorifying Himself. Scripture is not man-centered as though salvation were the main theme, but it is God-centered because His glory is the center. The Bible itself clearly teaches that salvation, important and wonderful as it is, is not an end in itself but is rather a means to the end of glorifying God. (Eph. 1:6, 12, 14). John F. Walvoord, Chafer's successor at Dallas Theological Seminary, puts it this way:

> ... the larger purpose of God is the manifestation of His own glory. To this end each dispensation, each succes-

[38]Cf. George E. Ladd, *The Blessed Hope* (Grand Rapids: Wm. B. Eerdmans Publishing Co., 1956), pp. 126-34. Even though Ladd believes in a future for the nation Israel (cf. "Is There a Future for Israel?" *Eternity*, May, 1964, pp. 25-28, 36), this does not mean that he is a dispensationalist, for he fails to meet this criterion concerning the consistent use of the literal principle of interpretation. In this same article (p. 27) he declares that "although the Church is spiritual Israel, the New Testament teaches that literal Israel is yet to be saved." In other words, he distinguishes the Church and Israel in the future millennial age, but he does not distinguish them in the present age. Since Israel and the Church are not kept distinct *throughout* God's program, Ladd fails to meet this test of dispensationalism too.
[39]Arnold B. Rhodes (ed.), *The Church Faces the Isms* (New York: Abingdon Press, 1958), p. 95.

sive revelation of God's plan for the ages, His dealing with the non-elect as with the elect . . . combine to manifest divine glory. . . .[40]

And in another place he says:

> All the events of the created world are designed to manifest the glory of God. The error of covenant theologians is that they combine all the many facets of divine purpose in the one objective of the fulfillment of the covenant of grace. From a logical standpoint, this is the reductive error—the use of one aspect of the whole as the determining element.[41]

The essence of dispensationalism, then, is the distinction between Israel and the Church. This grows out of the dispensationalist's consistent employment of normal or plain interpretation, and it reflects an understanding of the basic purpose of God in all His dealings with mankind as that of glorifying Himself through salvation and other purposes as well.

[40]John F. Walvoord, Review of *Crucial Questions About the Kingdom of God*, by George E. Ladd, *Bibliotheca Sacra*, 110 (January, 1953), 3-4.
[41]John F. Walvoord, *The Millennial Kingdom* (Findlay, Ohio: Dunham Publishing Co., 1959), p. 92.

3

WHAT ARE THE DISPENSATIONS?

THE NUMBER OF DISPENSATIONS

A. The Importance of the Question

IN THE PREVIOUS CHAPTER we have seen that covenant theologians (such as Hodge and Berkhof) list four and five dispensations in their concept of the outworking of the covenant of grace. This points to the fact that recognizing dispensations does not automatically make a man a dispensationalist. The essence of dispensationalism is (1) the recognition of a distinction between Israel and the Church, (2) a consistently literal principle of interpretation, and (3) a basic and working conception of the purpose of God as His own glory rather than as the single purpose of salvation.

On the basis of these statements and conclusions, it would follow that the number of dispensations in a dispensational scheme and even the names of the dispensations are relatively minor matters. Presumably one could have four, five, seven, or eight dispensations and be a consistent dispensationalist as long as the scheme is true to the three essentials of dispensationalism. Some opponents of dispensationalism recognize that these matters of number and name are relatively minor. Fuller, for instance, admits that "the number or names of the dispensations to which one holds is not essential to Dispensationalism . . ."[1] Others, like Bowman, use numbers to imply

---

[1]Daniel P. Fuller, "The Hermeneutics of Dispensationalism" (Doctor's dissertation, Northern Baptist Theological Seminary, Chicago, 1957), p. 23.

that the system is wrong because it teaches seven dispensations when the Bible connects only two with the word itself.[2] Seven is generally the number of dispensations most hold to, but that does not make the system five-sevenths wrong, if Bowman's implications be allowed. Suppose there were a dispensationalist who held to three dispensations. Then by Bowman's inference he would be two-thirds right.

However, in general, it seems to make very little difference to opponents of dispensationalism how many dispensations the dispensationalist has in his system after he goes beyond two. Two is the dividing line, for most covenant theologians hold to two at least and vigorously object to more. And yet even the covenant theologians are not quite sure what the two are. They may on occasion ridicule the fact that dispensationalists cannot agree on the number in their scheme, but they should realize that they are not united themselves. As has been pointed out, Berkhof equates the two basic dispensations with the Old and New Testaments. (Incidentally, such designations as "Old Dispensation" and "New Dispensation" are not Scriptural names!) More recently, Ernest F. Kevan, Principal of London (England) Bible College, is just as sure that the two dispensations are the Mosaic law and grace. Both of these he sees as the outworking of the single covenant of grace:

> God's covenanted purpose with sinful man has ever been one of grace; but the covenant of grace was based on a double plan, or to use scriptural terminology, was revealed in two dispensations. The first of these was the Mosaic dispensation, sometimes called the "Old Covenant," and the second is the Christian dispensation, usually called the "New Covenant." Strictly the covenant (q.v.) is one and the same covenant of grace.[3]

[2]John Wick Bowman, "The Bible and Modern Religions: II. Dispensationalism," *Interpretation*, 10 (April, 1956), 175.
[3]Ernest F. Kevan, "Dispensation," *Baker's Dictionary of Theology* (Grand Rapids: Baker Book House, 1960), p. 168.

Two—whatever they be called—are the limit for covenant theologians (though the Old is usually subdivided further by covenant theologians), and when a dispensationalist goes beyond two it makes little difference even to the covenant theologian how many more he has.

Nonetheless the question of how many dispensations there are is a very pertinent and practical one and worthy of consideration. Though it is not determinative, it is a part of the dispensational presentation.

B. Some Answers to the Question

Most dispensationalists see seven dispensations in God's plan (though throughout the history of dispensationalism they have not always been the same seven). Occasionally a dispensationalist may hold as few as four, and some hold as many as eight. The doctrinal statement of the Dallas Theological Seminary mentions only three by name (the Mosaic Law, the present dispensation of Grace, and the future dispensation of the Millennial Kingdom.)[4] Why is there this difference? Probably the answer lies in the fact that the three, Law, Grace, and Kingdom, are the subject of much of the material in the Bible, while the others, however many there may be, are not. In other words, the difference of opinion as to number is not due to a defect in the dispensational scheme but rather is due to lack of detailed revelation concerning the earliest periods of Biblical history. We do not have preserved in the written record all that God may have said or revealed to man in those early periods.

Nevertheless, on the basis of the definition of a dispensation as a distinguishable economy in the outworking of God's purpose, it is not difficult to deduce how many dispensations are revealed in Scripture.

If one is a premillennialist, then the distinguishable econ-

[4]Article V.

omy of God in the millennium, during which Christ is visibly present, is easily recognized. This present dispensation whose principal, not exclusive, characteristic is grace also is easily justified by the definition. The same is apparent with the Mosaic dispensation of the Law, and the point need not be labored. It is the time between the beginning of creation to the giving of the law that gives rise in some minds to the question of the validity of all the dispensations which are said to belong to that period. However, before the Fall of man the arrangement was certainly distinguishably different from that after the Fall.

Already we have accounted for five dispensations: (1) pre-Fall, (2) whatever name should be given to that which obtained after the Fall to the time of Moses, (3) the Law, (4) Grace, and (5) the Millennial Kingdom. The very fact that it is difficult to find a suitable name to cover the entire economy from the Fall to Moses ought to make one examine carefully the validity of trying to view that entire period as having only one dispensation. It should be apparent that up to the time of Abraham God's administration concerned all nations, whereas with Abraham He began to single out one nation, and in the singling out He made a very distinctive covenant with Abraham. Therefore, the distinguishable characteristic of God's dealing with Abraham in promise seems sufficient to delineate what is often called the dispensation of Promise.

The only question that remains is whether or not the dispensations which are popularly called Conscience and Government are valid. Suppose there was only one dispensation during that period, what is it to be called? If there were two, what were the distinguishing features that justify two? The problem is complicated by the fact that the revelation of Scripture covering this long period is very brief. It seems that there is sufficient warrant in God's new arrangement for human government in the time of Noah to distinguish a dispensation at that time (cf. Gen. 9:6 with 4:15). If this be agreed with, then there are seven dispensations, and one must admit that the more one studies in the light of a basic definition, the more inclined he is to conclude that there are seven dispensations. It seems to be somewhat fashionable these days to avoid this conclusion or at least to minimize the earlier dispensations, but if one has a consistently workable definition and if one applies it throughout all history, then it seems hard not to arrive at seven.

SOME QUESTIONS

Some further questions arise in relation to what seems to be the sevenfold dispensational picture in Scripture. These are questions, not problems, and they in no way affect the system as a whole. They are in no way basic, but they are interesting to consider, and therefore we do so.

A. THE NOAHIC ECONOMY

In viewing the usual Scofield outline, a question arises revolving around the matter of distinguishing what he calls the dispensations of Conscience (from the Fall to Noah) and of Government (from Noah to Abraham). It is quite plausible to consider that Noah lived under the basic stewardship responsibilities instituted after the Fall of man. One of the author's students once suggested that this entire period be called the dispensation of Justice, since this was the distinctive revelation of God in His relationship with man during that time.

Yet, on the other hand, some distinct and new arrangements were instituted with Noah and mankind after the Flood. To be specific, four are recorded in Genesis 9:1-17. (1) A fear of man is put in the heart of the animals (v. 2). (2) Man is permitted to eat the flesh of animals, whereas prior to that time apparently he was a vegetarian (v. 3). (3)

The principle of capital punishment is instituted (v. 6). (4) God binds Himself to a promise of never causing another flood on the earth (vv. 8-17). When one views these four arrangements with man after the Flood, they seem to mark off a new economy from God's viewpoint, a new responsibility from man's, and they certainly constitute new truth in the progress of revelation. Therefore, they apparently mark off a new dispensation. Whether or not the title "Human Government" is the best is not the point at the moment.

B. The Eternal State

Another question that has arisen in some writings is whether or not the eternal state is to be considered a dispensation.[5] Most commentaries that are not premillennial refer the phrase "the dispensation of the fullness of times" (Eph. 1:10) to the present gospel age, while those that are premillennial refer it to the millennial kingdom.[6] However, it would seem from the concept of a dispensation as related to God's running the affairs of His household, the world, that when temporal history ends, the household arrangement, which is the basis for a dispensational stewardship, also ends. In other words, the dispensational economies are related to the affairs of this world, and they are no longer needed when the world ends. Thus in eternity there is no need for the economic relationships of a dispensation.

C. The Mosaic Law

Another question concerns the Mosaic Law. This dispensation was operative over a long period of time if it was inaugurated with Moses and continued until the crucifixion of Christ. During that extended period Israel's change in spiritual condition might seem to indicate a change in dispensa-

[5]As William Evans, *Outline Study of the Bible* (Chicago: Moody Press, 1913), pp.30-37.
[6]Cf. L. S. Chafer, *The Ephesian Letter* (New York: Loizeaux Brothers, 1935), pp. 49-50.

tion. Specifically, when God sent His message through the prophets, did He change the dispensational relationship? The answer to this question will not be found by examining the prophets' messages, but in looking at the relationship of the Lord Jesus to the Mosaic law during His lifetime. For if He considered the law still operative and incumbent on the Jewish people, then it could not have been abrogated or replaced by the message of the prophets. If the Mosaic law was still the operating principle during Christ's lifetime, then the dispensation of the Law did not end until the cross.

Of course it is not difficult to show that Christ lived under the law and that He expected His hearers to follow its teachings too. When He cleansed the leper He told him to present himself to the priest "and offer the gift that Moses commanded . . ." (Matt. 8:2-4). He further exhorted the people to obey the commands of the law as they were taught them by the scribes and Pharisees, but not to follow the examples of their lives (Matt. 23:2-3). He also declared that He did not come to destroy the law (Matt. 5:17). This statement would mean nothing if the law had been superseded by a dispensation of the Prophets.

D. The Tribulation

But the most difficult and important question to answer is that which concerns the distinctiveness of the Tribulation period. In relation to the usual dispensational scheme, there are three possible views as to how the Tribulation period fits in.

First, Chafer suggested that the period will be akin to the Mosaic law and will include a revival of the principles of that economy.[7] For instance, the Sabbath day will apparently be observed strictly during the period (Matt. 24:20). Furthermore, it will be a time when God will deal specially with

[7] L. S. Chafer, *Major Bible Themes* (Chicago: Moody Press, 1942), p. 100.

Israel again. It is the seventieth week of Daniel, and since the first sixty-nine weeks were part of the economy of the law, it must be also.

The principal objection to this view is simply that no other dispensation comes back into effect again once it has ended, and there is no question that the Mosaic law ended with the first advent of Christ (Rom. 10:4). It would be a very unusual thing to reinstitute a dispensation after a lapse of two thousand years or more. Of course, God could do that, but it would seem to be more natural to consider the Tribulation as a distinct dispensation with similarities to the Mosaic economy.

And that is the second possible view—the Tribulation is a distinguishable economy in the outworking of God's purpose. In the scheme usually presented, it would then become the seventh of eight dispensations.[8] There are many characteristics to commend such a view. The Tribulation is above all a time of wrath, not grace; it distinctly deals with Israel again; assuming the rapture before the Tribulation, the true Church is absent from the earth; and the gospel to be preached during that period is the gospel of the kingdom (Matt. 24:14). These features seem to characterize a different dispensation.

But these are not the only considerations. To be sure, the Sabbath will be observed during that time, but by whom? By those Jewish people who find themselves in their land again and who are attempting to set up their ancient worship once more. They do this in self-will, not because they are obeying the responsibilities of a Tribulation economy which includes worship on the Sabbath as a requirement. After all, many Jews today both in and out of Palestine observe the Sabbath, but this does not mean we are no longer under the dispensation of Grace. God has not ordained this observance for to-

[8]As Evans, *op. cit.*, and Clarence E. Mason, "Eschatology" (mimeographed notes, Philadelphia College of Bible, 1962), pp. 52-54.

day, nor will He in the Tribulation period; therefore, its observance does not indicate a dispensational change.

To be sure, it will be a period of the outpouring of the wrath of God. But it will also be a time of much salvation. Many Jews and multitudes of Gentiles will come to know the Lord (Rev. 7). So it will be a time during which grace will not be absent but rather very manifestly present. Even if one makes a distinction between the gospel of the grace of God and the gospel of the kingdom, this does not mean that the gospel of the kingdom will not include the message of the cross. It will add the aspect of good news which announces the coming kingdom along with the message of the cross. Too, the gospel of the kingdom was preached by the Lord during His earthly ministry (Matt. 4:17) while the dispensation of the law was still operative. Thus the preaching of the gospel of the kingdom was not then, nor will it be later, a distinctive enough difference to mark off a new dispensation.

The same is true of the argument based on the seventy weeks. They are not distinctive of a dispensation. After all, they began about a thousand years after the law was given Israel, and even though God turns His attention to Israel again during the Tribulation, He does not do this to the exclusion of others. In other words, the fact that time is being reckoned according to the chronology of the seventy weeks was not distinctive to the Law economy and does not necessarily need to distinguish the Tribulation as an economy.

Therefore, it seems that the Tribulation with its many judgments is from the dispensational viewpoint the end of the economy of Grace. This is the third view. From the viewpoint of the seventy weeks for Israel it is their last week. From the viewpoint of the true Church there is no relation, since the Church will be raptured before the Tribulation begins. But from the dispensational viewpoint of God's running the affairs of the world, it seems more natural to consider the

Tribulation as that time when He is bringing to a conclusion the economy of Grace with judgments on men who have rejected Him, rather than to consider it a separate dispensation. The Church is not subject to the judgments, just as Noah was not judged by the flood in his day. But in both cases the dispensation does not end until the judgments are completed.

Remember, these questions are minor in relation to the main tenets of dispensationalism. The fact that there are questions is not the fault of the system but is due to lack of detailed revelation, and differing answers to these questions will not make or break the system.

The matter of a dispensation to Paul, distinct from that which began at Pentecost, will be discussed in the chapter on ultradispensationalism.

THE NAMES AND CHARACTERISTICS OF
THE DISPENSATIONS

Again let it be said that a sevenfold scheme of dispensations is not inspired and authoritative. Nevertheless, one must have some scheme, and to this writer it seems difficult to get away from the concept of seven distinguishable economies of God. Using this picture, then, let us look at some of the characteristics of these economies.

A. THE DISPENSATION OF INNOCENCY OR FREEDOM

This first dispensation is usually called Innocency. Although this term is not a good description of Adam's condition before the Fall, it is probably the best single word. The word *innocent* is too neutral. Adam was not created merely innocent but with a positive holiness which enabled him to have face-to-face communication with God. Nevertheless, his holiness was not the same as the Creator's, for it was limited by virtue of Adam's being a creature. Too, his holiness was unconfirmed until he should successfully pass the test placed before him. Therefore, it seems that Adam's moral condition before God in those days of "innocency" was unconfirmed creaturely holiness. But that is too long a phrase for the name of a dispensation; therefore, we are back to calling it the dispensation of Innocency.

Nevin has a commendable suggestion, the dispensation of Freedom.[9] The word *freedom* does characterize the condition of man before he became a slave to sin, and as much as a creature can have freedom, Adam had it before sin enslaved his will.

In this economy the key person was Adam; indeed we ought to consider it a dispensation or stewardship to Adam (as all the dispensations from the human viewpoint are stewardships). His responsibilities involved maintaining the garden and not eating of the fruit of the tree of the knowledge of good and evil. He failed the test about eating, and as a result, far-reaching judgments were pronounced on him, his wife, mankind, and the creation. At the same time God pronounced judgment, He also graciously intervened, promised a Redeemer, and made immediate provision for the acceptability of Adam and Eve in their sinful condition before God.

The Scripture revelation concerning this economy is recorded in Genesis 1:28—3:6.

B. The Dispensation of Conscience or Self-determination

The average dispensationalist has been schooled to designate the second economy as Conscience. The title comes from Romans 2:15 and is a proper designation of the stewardship. The title does not imply that man had no conscience before or after this time, any more than the dispensation of Law (which even covenant theologians recognize) implies that there was no law before or after the period. It simply

[9]Paul David Nevin, "Some Major Problems in Dispensational Interpretation" (Doctor's dissertation, Dallas Theological Seminary, 1963), p. 111.

means that this was the principal way God governed mankind during this economy, and obedience to the dictates of conscience was man's chief stewardship responsibility.

Sauer suggests that this dispensation might be called the dispensation of "self-determination."[10] Mason calls it the dispensation of "Moral Responsibility."[11] These designations have much to commend them, but may not be sufficiently better than "Conscience" to try to reeducate the majority of dispensationalists who have been reared on the Scofield notes.

During this stewardship man was responsible to respond to God through the promptings of his conscience, and in his response he was to bring an acceptable blood sacrifice as God had taught him to do (Gen. 3:21; 4:4). We have a record of only a few responding, and Abel, Enoch, and Noah are especially cited as heroes of faith. We also have the record of those who did not respond and who by their evil deeds brought judgment on the world. Cain refused to acknowledge himself as a sinner even when God continued to admonish him (Gen. 4:3, 7). Murder came on the scene of human history. Unnatural affection was widespread (Gen. 6:2). Finally there was open violence and corruption and widespread evil desire and purpose of heart (Gen. 6:5). The long-suffering of God (I Pet. 3:20) came to an end, and He brought the Flood as judgment on the universal wickedness of man. But at the same time God graciously intervened, and Noah found grace (the first use of the word in the Bible) in His sight (Gen. 6:8), and he and his family were saved. The revelation of this economy is preserved in Genesis 4:1—8:14.

C. THE DISPENSATION OF CIVIL GOVERNMENT

The propriety of a new dispensation after the Flood has already been discussed. The chief personage during this

[10]Erich Sauer, *From Eternity to Eternity* (London: Paternoster Press, 1954), p. 21.
[11]Mason, *op. cit.*, p. 45a.

economy was Noah. The new revelation of this time included animals' fear of man, animals given to man to eat, the promise of no further floods, and the institution of capital punishment. It is this latter that gives the distinctive basis to this dispensation as that of Human or Civil Government. God gave man the right to take the life of man, which in the very nature of the case gave man the authority to govern others. Unless government has the right to the highest form of punishment, its basic authority is questionable and insufficient to protect properly those whom it governs.

Failure to govern successfully appeared on the scene almost immediately, for Noah became drunk and incapable of ruling. The people instead of obeying God's command to scatter and fill the earth conceived the idea of staying together and building the tower of Babel to help achieve their aim. Fellowship with man replaced fellowship with God. As a result, God sent the judgment of the tower of Babel and the confusion of languages. He also graciously intervened in that He did not utterly destroy the nations but chose to deal graciously with Abraham and his descendants. The Scriptural revelation of this stewardship is found in Genesis 8:15—11:9.

D. THE DISPENSATION OF PROMISE OR PATRIARCHAL RULE

The title *Promise* comes from Hebrews 6:15 and 11:9 where it is said that Abraham obtained the promise and sojourned in the land of promise. The title emphasizes the revelation of the economy. The governmental feature of the economy is best emphasized by the designation dispensation of Patriarchal Rule. Until this dispensation, all mankind had been *directly* related to God's governing principles. Now God marked out one family and one nation and in them made a representative test of all.

The responsibility of the patriarchs was simply to believe and serve God, and God gave them every material and spirit-

ual provision to encourage them to do this. The promised
land was theirs and blessing was theirs as long as they remained in the land. But of course there was failure soon and
often. Finally Jacob led the people to Egypt and soon the
judgment of slavery was brought on them. But God again
graciously provided a deliverer and in the process of deliver-
ance killed their oppressors. The Scripture involved in this
dispensation is Genesis 11:10—Exodus 18:27.

Is this a dispensation distinct from that of the Mosaic Law
or is it merely a preparatory period? The answer seems to be
clear from Galatians 3:15-29. Though it is true that God was
dealing with the same people during both the Patriarchal
and Mosaic dispensations, this is not the determining factor.
After all, up to the call of Abraham, God had been dealing
in different ways with the same group—the entire population
of the earth. In the first and second dispensations God was
dealing with the same people—Adam and Eve. So the fact
that he was dealing with Israel during both the Patriarchal
and legal eras is not determinative. What does determine the
distinguishability of the two dispensations is simply the different bases on which He dealt with them. Promise and Law
are sharply distinguished by Paul in Galatians 3 even though
he maintains that the law did not annul the promise. And
the Mosaic Law is kept so distinct from the promise to Abraham that it is difficult not to recognize a different dispensation. This is the essence of the definition, and if anything is
kept distinct in that chapter, the law is. Therefore, the separate dispensation of Promise or of the Patriarchs is justified.

E. THE DISPENSATION OF THE MOSAIC LAW

To the children of Israel through Moses was given the
great code that we call the Mosaic law. It consisted of 613
commandments covering all phases of life and activity. It
revealed in specific detail God's will in that economy. The

period covered was from Moses until the death of Christ, or from Exodus 19:1 to Acts 1:26.

The people were responsible to do all the law (Jas. 2:10), but they failed (Rom. 10:1-3). As a result, there were many judgments throughout this long period. The ten tribes were carried into Assyrian captivity; the two tribes were carried into Babylonian captivity; and later, because of their rejection of Jesus of Nazareth, the people were dispersed into all the world (Matt. 23:37-39). All during their many periods of declension and backsliding, God dealt with them graciously from the very first apostasy with the golden calf when the law was being delivered to Moses, to the gracious promises of final regathering and restoration in the millennial age to come. These promises of a glorious future are guaranteed secure by the Abrahamic promises, which the law in no way abrogated (Gal. 3:3-25). We are also told very clearly in the New Testament (Rom. 3:20) that the law was not a means of justification but of condemnation. Its relation to salvation and the dispensationalist's view of salvation under the law will be discussed later.

F. THE DISPENSATION OF GRACE

The Apostle Paul was principally, though not exclusively, the agent of the revelation of the grace of God for this dispensation. Christ Himself brought the grace of God to mankind in His incarnation (Titus 2:11), but Paul was the one who expounded it. To be sure the dispensationalist does not say that there was no grace ever displayed before the coming of Christ (any more than he says there is no law after His coming), but the Scriptures do say that His coming displayed the grace of God in such brightness that all previous displays could be considered as nothing.

Under Grace the responsibility on man is to accept the gift of righteousness which God freely offers to all (Rom. 5:15-

18). There are two aspects of the grace of God in this economy: (1) the blessing is entirely of grace and (2) that grace is for all. God is no longer dealing with just one nation as a sample but with all mankind. The vast majority have rejected Him and as a result will be judged. The dispensation will end at the second coming of Christ since, as suggested, the Tribulation period itself is not a separate dispensation but is the judgment on those living persons who are Christ rejectors at the end of this present dispensation. The Scripture involved is Acts 2:1 to Revelation 19:21.

G. THE DISPENSATION OF THE MILLENNIUM

After the second advent of Christ the millennial kingdom will be set up in fulfillment of all the promises given in both Testaments and particularly those contained in the Abrahamic and Davidic covenants. The Lord Jesus Christ, who will personally take charge of the running of the affairs of the world during that age, will be the chief personage of the dispensation. It will continue for a thousand years, and man will be responsible for obedience to the King and His laws. Satan will be bound, Christ will be ruling, righteousness will prevail, overt disobedience will be quickly punished. Yet at the end of the period enough rebels will be found to make a formidable army which will dare to attack the seat of government (Rev. 20:7-9). The revolt will be unsuccessful and the rebels will be cast into everlasting punishment.

This is a survey of what the dispensations are. But there is one other answer to this question of the chapter that is a very important and often overlooked consideration. The dispensations are likely seven in number; they can be designated as we have suggested; they exhibit certain characteristics. But above all, dispensations are stewardships, and each stewardship has its stewards. One man usually stands out particularly at the beginning of each dispensation, and with the exception of the first and last dispensations that chief personage does not live throughout the period covered. The stewardship responsibility, therefore, is not restricted to one man but in some sense is placed on all who live under the economy.

Let us relate this idea to the dispensation of Grace. Though Paul was a chief agent of revelation of the grace of God, many others are stewards under the economy. The other apostles and prophets (Eph. 3:5) and all believers (I Pet. 4:10) are also stewards of that grace. This means for every Christian a personal involvement in the grace of God. It is not as if we are spectators sitting in the audience watching the grace of God play on the stage. We are participants in the drama and, more than that, we have a lead role in witnessing to and displaying the grace of God under this stewardship. A dispensational responsibility means involvement for those who respond to the principles of the administration. The same responsibility means judgment for those who reject its principles.[12]

---

[12]Erich Sauer, who has been an able contributor to dispensational thought, also holds to seven dispensations exactly as outlined in this chapter. The only difference in his scheme has been noted, i. e., he calls the second dispensation that of "Self-determination." He relates these periods to the history of salvation in the unfolding progress of revelation. Cf. *From Eternity to Eternity*, p. 24.

4

THE ORIGINS OF DISPENSATIONALISM

A TYPICAL STATEMENT about dispensationalism goes like this: "Dispensationalism was formulated by one of the nineteenth-century separatist movements, the Plymouth Brethren."[1] This is a loaded statement. It contains two charges: (1) Since dispensationalism is recent, it is therefore unorthodox. (2) It was born out of a separatist movement and is therefore to be shunned. The implication in these charges is clear: If the poor misguided souls who believe in dispensationalism only knew its true origin they would turn from its teachings like the plague. If that sounds too sarcastic, then listen to this statement by Fuller:

> Ignorance is bliss, and it may well be that this popularity would not be so great if the adherents of this system knew the historical background of what they teach. Few indeed realize that the teaching of Chafer came from Scofield, who in turn got it through the writings of Darby and the Plymouth Brethren.[2]

A further implication in a statement like Fuller's is that dispensationalism is obviously man-made, and a person would never arrive at such ideas from his own personal Bible study.

[1] E. J. Carnell, *The Case for Orthodox Theology* (Philadelphia: Westminster Press, 1959), p. 117.
[2] Daniel P. Fuller, "The Hermeneutics of Dispensationalism" (Doctor's dissertation, Northern Baptist Theological Seminary, Chicago, 1957), p. 136.

The idea came from Darby through Scofield and Chafer, and certainly not from the Bible.

THE CHARGE OF RECENCY

A. STRAW MEN

In discussing the matter of the origins of dispensationalism, opponents of the teaching usually set up two straw men and then huff and puff until they are destroyed. The first is the straw man of saying that dispensationalists assert that the *system* was taught in post-apostolic times. Informed dispensationalists do not claim that. They recognize that as a system dispensationalism was largely formulated by Darby, but that outlines of a dispensationalist approach to the Scriptures are found much earlier. They only maintain that certain features of the dispensational system are found in the teaching of the early church.

Another typical example of the use of a straw man is this line of argument: pretribulationalism is not apostolic; pretribulationalism is dispensationalism; therefore, dispensationalism is not apostolic.[3] But dispensationalists do not claim that the system was developed in the first century; nor is it necessary that they be able to do so. Many other doctrines were not developed in the first century—including covenant theology which is seventeenth century. Doctrinal development is a perfectly normal process in the course of church history.

This straw man leads to a second fallacy—the wrong use of history. The fact that something was taught in the first century does not make it right (unless taught in the canonical Scriptures), and the fact that something was not taught until the nineteenth century does not make it wrong unless, of course, it is unscriptural. Nondispensationalists surely know

[3]C. B. Bass, *Backgrounds to Dispensationalism* (Grand Rapids: Wm. B. Eerdmans Publishing Co., 1960), pp. 39-43.

that baptismal regeneration was taught in the early centuries and yet many of them would not include that error in their theological systems simply because it is historic. After all, the ultimate question is not, Is dispensationalism—or any other teaching—historic? but, Is it Scriptural? Most opponents of dispensationalism realize that this is the issue, but they still persist in using the historical argument with its fallacious implications. Bass' entire book is a good example of such an unscholarly approach. He devotes two sentences to the recognition of the fact that the test is Scripture, not history,[4] and he devotes most of the remainder of the book testing dispensationalism by history and by Darby's personal church activities.

The charge of newness was leveled long ago at the doctrine of the Reformers. Calvin answered it with characteristic straightforwardness, and his answer is one which defends dispensationalism equally well against the same charge. He wrote: "First, by calling it 'new' they do great wrong to God, whose Sacred Word does not deserve to be accused of novelty. . . . That it has lain long unknown and buried is the fault of man's impiety. Now when it is restored to us by God's goodness, its claim to *antiquity* ought to be admitted at least by right of recovery."[5]

B. Unsystematized Dispensationalism or Early Dispensational Concepts

It is granted by dispensationalists that as a system of theology dispensationalism is recent in origin. But there are historical references to that which eventually was systematized into dispensationalism. There is evidence in the writings of men who lived long before Darby that the dispensational concept was a part of their viewpoint. If this be true, then it

[4]*Ibid.*, p. 47.
[5]John Calvin, *Institutes of the Christian Religion*, "Prefatory Address to King Francis," p. 3.

would scarcely be scholarly to say, as one opponent of dispensationalism does:

> It is not important for the present purpose to determine whether the views of Darby and Kelly were original with them or were taken over from their antecedents and made popular by them. Sources to solve this historical problem are not available to the present writer. For all practical purposes, we may consider that this movement —for dispensationalism has had such wide influence that it must be called a movement—had its source with Darby and Kelly.[6]

Sources are available and have been available for many years. The writings of the Church Fathers were in print long before Ladd was born, and Ehlert's excellent work, "A Bibliography of Dispensationalism," was in print several years before Ladd's book was published.[7] At any rate, evidence is available and shows that dispensational concepts were held early and throughout the history of the church.

Justin Martyr (110-165) held a concept of differing programs of God. In the *Dialogue with Trypho,* in discussing the subject that God always taught the same righteousness, he said:

> For if one should wish to ask you why, since Enoch, Noah with his sons, and all others in similar circumstances, who neither were circumcised nor kept the Sabbath, pleased God, God demanded by other leaders and by the giving of the law after the lapse of so many generations, that those who lived between the times of Abraham and of Moses be justified by circumcision and the other ordinances—to wit, the Sabbath, and sacrifices, and libations, and offerings. . . .[8]

[6]George E. Ladd, *Crucial Questions About the Kingdom of God* (Grand Rapids: Wm. B. Eerdmans Publishing Co., 1952), p. 49.
[7]Arnold H. Ehlert, "A Bibliography of Dispensationalism," *Bibliotheca Sacra,* 101:95-101; 199-209; 319-28; 447-60; 102:84-92; 207-19; 322-34; 455-67; 103:57-67 (January, 1944, through January, 1946).
[8]XCII.

Earlier in the same work he spoke of the present dispensation and of its gifts of power.[9]

Irenaeus (130-200) wrote of reasons why there are only four Gospels. One of them is as follows:

> . . . and the Gospel is quadriform, as is also the course followed by the Lord. For this reason were four principal covenants given to the human race: one, prior to the deluge, under Adam; the second, that after the deluge, under Noah; the third, the giving of the law, under Moses; the fourth, that which renovates man, and sums up all things in itself by means of the Gospel, raising and bearing men upon its wings into the heavenly kingdom.[10]

He did not call these periods dispensations in this place, though he often spoke of the dispensations of God and especially of the Christian dispensation.

Clement of Alexandria (150-220) distinguished three patriarchal dispensations (in Adam, Noah, and Abraham) as well as the Mosaic. Samuel Hanson Coxe (1793-1880) backed up his own sevenfold dispensational scheme by Clement's fourfold one.[11]

Augustine also reflects these early dispensational concepts in his writings. Although his oft-quoted statement, "Distinguish the times, and the Scripture is in harmony with itself," does not in its context apply to dispensational ideas, he elsewhere makes some applicable statements.

> The divine institution of sacrifice was suitable in the former dispensation, but is not suitable now. For the change suitable to the present age has been enjoined by God, who knows infinitely better than man what is fitting for every age, and who is, whether He give or add, abolish or curtail, increase or diminish, the unchange-

[9]LXXXVII.
[10]*Against Heresies*, III, XI, 8.
[11]A. C. Coxe (ed.), *The Ante-Nicene Fathers*, II, 476.

able Creator of mutable things, ordering all events in
His providence until the beauty of the completed course
of time, the component parts of which are the dispensations adapted to each successive age, shall be finished,
like the grand melody of some ineffably wise master of
song, and those pass into the eternal immediate contem-
plation of God who here, though it is a time of faith, not
of sight, are acceptably worshipping Him. . . . There is
no variableness with God, though in the former period
of the world's history He enjoined one kind of offerings,
and in the latter period another, therein ordering the
symbolical actions pertaining to the blessed doctrine of
true religion in harmony with the changes of successive
epochs without any change in Himself.
. . . if it is now established that that which was for one
age rightly ordained may be in another age rightly
changed,—the alteration indicating a change in the work,
not in the plan, of Him who makes the change, the plan
being framed by His reasoning faculty, to which, uncon-
ditioned by succession in time, those things are simul-
taneously present which cannot be actually done at the
same time because the ages succeed each other.[12]

It is not suggested nor should it be inferred that these early
Church Fathers were dispensationalists in the modern sense
of the word. But it is true that some of them enunciated
principles which later developed into dispensationalism, and
it may be rightly said that they held to primitive or early dispensational concepts.

From this time until after the Reformation there were no
substantial contributions to that which was later systematized
as dispensationalism. After important doctrinal issues of the
Reformation were settled, theologians were able to turn their
attention again to these matters involving God's dealing with
man.

[12]*To Marcellinus,* CXXXVIII, 5, 7.

C. Developing Dispensationalism or the Period Before Darby

Pierre Poiret was a French mystic and philosopher (1646-1719). His great work, *L'OEconomie Divine,* first published in Amsterdam in 1687, was translated into English and published in London in six volumes in 1713. The work began as a development of the doctrine of predestination, but was expanded into a rather complete systematic theology. In viewpoint it is sometimes mystical, represents a modified form of Calvinism, and is premillennial and dispensational. Each of the six volumes is devoted to a particular economy, though his dispensational scheme does not exactly follow the title of each volume. The scheme as set forth in these volumes is as follows:

I. Infancy—to the Deluge
II. Childhood—to Moses
III. Adolescence—to the prophets (about the time of Solomon)
IV. Youth—to the coming of Christ
V. Manhood—"some time after that"
VI. Old Age—"the time of man's decay"
    (V and VI seem to be the early and latter part of the Christian dispensation.)
VII. Renovation of all things—the millennium[13]

Ehlert correctly assesses the importance of this man's work as follows:

> There is no question that we have here a genuine dispensational scheme. He uses the phrase "period or dispensation" and his seventh dispensation is a literal thousand-year millennium with Christ returned and reigning in bodily form upon the earth with His saints, and Israel regathered and converted. He sees the over-

[13]Peter Poiret, *The Divine OEconomy: or An Universal System of the Works and Purposes of God Towards Men Demonstrated* (London: 1713).

throw of corrupt Protestantism, the rise of Antichrist, the two resurrections, and many of the general run of end-time events. . . .[14]

John Edwards (1639-1716) published in 1699 two volumes, totaling about 790 pages, entitled *A Compleat History or Survey of All the Dispensations*. His purpose in the books was "to display all the Transactions of Divine Providence relating to the Methods of Religion, from the Creation to the end of the World, from the first Chapter of Genesis to the last of the Revelation."[15] He believed in a millennium, but he understood it to be a spiritual reign. "I conceive," he said, "He may Personally Appear above, though He will not Reign Personally on Earth."[16] His dispensational scheme was as follows:

    I. Innocency and Felicity, or Adam created upright
   II. Sin and Misery, Adam fallen
  III. Reconciliation, or Adam recovered, from Adam's redemption to the end of the world
      A. Patriarchal economy
        1. Adamical, antediluvian
        2. Noahical
        3. Abrahamick
      B. Mosaical
      C. Gentile (concurrent with A and B)
      D. Christian or Evangelical
        1. Infancy, primitive period, past
        2. Childhood, present period
        3. Manhood, future (millennium)
        4. Old age, from the loosing of Satan to the conflagration

[14]Ehlert, *op. cit.*, 101:449-50.
[15]John Edwards, *A Compleat History or Survey of All the Dispensations and Methods of Religion*, I, v.
[16]*Ibid.*, II, 720.

Isaac Watts (1674-1748), best known as a hymn writer, was also a theologian (with Arian tendencies) whose writings fill six large volumes. In a forty-page essay entitled "The Harmony of all the Religions which God ever Prescribed to Men and all his Dispensations towards them," he defined his concept of dispensations and presented his system. His definition is as follows:

> The public *dispensations* of God towards men, are those wise and holy constitutions of his will and government, revealed or some way manifested to them, in the several successive periods or *ages* of the world, wherein are contained the duties which he expects from men, and the blessings which he promises, or encourages them to expect from him, here and hereafter; together with the sins which he forbids, and the punishments which he threatens to inflict on such sinners, or the *dispensations* of God may be described more briefly, as the appointed moral rules of God's dealing with mankind, considered as reasonable creatures, and as accountable to him for their behaviour, both in this world and in that which is to come. Each of these dispensations of God, may be represented as different religions, or at least, as different forms of religion, appointed for men in the several *successive ages* of the world.[17]

His dispensational outline is as follows:

I. The Dispensation of Innocency, or the Religion of Adam at first
II. The Adamical Dispensation of the Covenant of Grace, or the Religion of Adam after his Fall
III. The Noahical Dispensation, or the Religion of Noah
IV. The Abrahamical Dispensation, or the Religion of Abraham
V. The Mosaical Dispensation, or the Jewish Religion

[17]Watts' *Works*, II, 625 (Leeds ed.), II, 543 (London ed.).

VI. The Christian Dispensation

Except for the exclusion of the millennium (he did not consider it a dispensation), this outline is exactly like that in the
Scofield Reference Bible, and it is Watts' outline, not Darby's!
Thus throughout this period there was significant thinking
and considerable literature on the subject of God's dealings
with mankind throughout the ages. This was a period of
developing dispensationalism.

D. Systematized Dispensationalism or Darby to
the Present

There is no question that the Plymouth Brethren, of which
John Nelson Darby (1800-1882) was a leader, had much to do
with the systematizing and promoting of dispensationalism.
But neither Darby nor the Brethren originated the concepts
involved in the system, and even if they had that would not
make them wrong if they can be shown to be Biblical.

Darby was born in London of Irish parents, was educated
at Trinity College, Dublin (from which he graduated at the
age of eighteen), and was admitted to the bar at the age of
twenty-two. He was converted and abandoned his legal ca-
reer after one year and was ordained in the Church of England. He worked vigorously and with remarkable success in
his first parish, with the result that at one time Roman Cath-
olics were "becoming Protestants at the rate of 600 to 800 a
week."[18]

Because of the alliance of the Church of England with the
state, Darby soon felt that he must leave that ministry and
seek a fellowship which emphasized a more spiritual and
intimate communion. He began to meet with a group of
people who belonged to the Church of England in Dublin
and who because of their dissatisfaction with that church
were seeking more personal communion and Bible study.

[18]For documentation see Bass, *op. cit.*, p. 50.

These early meetings were begun before Darby became dissatisfied. He was not the founder of this group, and the meetings were in no way a protest but rather a spontaneous gathering.

After some traveling, Darby settled in Plymouth, England, where in 1831 the breaking-of-bread service was begun. By 1840 there were some eight hundred people attending these services and it was inevitable that the group, whom Darby had insisted should be known not by any denominational name but simply as brethren, would be called Plymouth Brethren. Many groups subsequently sprang up in Britain and later in other parts of the world. Darby himself spread the movement by his own travels to Germany, Italy, the United States, and New Zealand. He was an indefatigable worker. His written ministry incorporates some forty volumes of six hundred pages each, including a translation of the Bible. His works show a breadth of scholarship in his knowledge of the Biblical languages, philosophy, and ecclesiastical history. The early assemblies had their problems, and Darby figures largely in the disputes of those years.[19]

Darby's dispensational scheme (though not always easily discerned from his writings) was as follows:

    I. Paradisaical state to the Flood
   II. Noah
  III. Abraham
  IV. Israel
      A. Under the law
      B. Under the priesthood
      C. Under the kings
   V. Gentiles
  VI. The Spirit
 VII. The Millennium[20]

[19]Cf. Bass, *op. cit.*, pp. 48-99. His factual account of the life and ministry of Darby is excellent, though his inferential conclusions are not always so.

[20]*The Collected Writings of J. N. Darby* (London: G. Morrish, 1867), II, 568-73.

His philosophy of dispensationalism is stated in the following words:

> This however we have to learn in its details, in the various dispensations which led to or have followed the revelations of the incarnate Son in whom all the fulness was pleased to dwell. . . . The detail of the history connected with these dispensations brings out many most interesting displays, both of the principles and patience of God's dealing with the evil and failure of man; and of the workings by which He formed faith on His own thus developed perfections. But the dispensations themselves all declare some leading principle or interference of God, some condition in which He has placed man, principles which in themselves are everlastingly sanctioned of God, but in the course of those dispensations placed responsibly in the hands of man for the display and discovery of what he was, and the bringing in their infallible establishment in Him to whom the glory of them all rightly belonged . . . . in every instance, there was total and immediate failure as regarded man, however the patience of God might tolerate and carry on by grace the dispensation in which man has thus failed in the outset; and further, that there is no instance of the restoration of a dispensation afforded us, though there might be partial revivals of it through faith.[21]

Only one comment is necessary concerning Darby's teachings—it was obviously not the pattern which Scofield followed. If Scofield parroted anybody's scheme it was Watts', not Darby's. Although we cannot minimize the wide influence of Darby, the glib statement that dispensationalism originated with Darby, whose system was taken over and popularized by Scofield, is not historically accurate.

[21]*Ibid.*, I, 192-93.

E. The Progress of Dogma

Our findings about the relative recency of systematic dispensationalism should not be surprising. It would not be unexpected that a subject whose primary distinctions have to do with eschatology should not have been systematized until eschatology began to be refined seriously by the church. Most agree that the history of dogma has followed a certain pattern of unfolding development and discussion. Orr, in his classic work *The Progress of Dogma,* shows how the doctrines taken up for theological study by the church throughout her history chronologically correspond with the general order followed in most systematic theologies. In chronological order the doctrinal discussions were on apologetics, theology proper, anthropology, Christology, soteriology, and, after the Reformation, eschatology.[22] Undoubtedly the recency of systematic eschatology partly accounts for the relative recency of systematic dispensationalism. This is not to say that eschatology or even a primitive dispensationalism was not considered before post-Reformation times, but it is to say that systematic development of doctrine in these areas was delayed until then. Thus the toil of eschatological study has borne the good fruit of dispensational distinctions in this modern period of the progress of dogma.

To sum up: In answer to the charge that dispensationalism is recent and therefore suspect, we have tried to show two things: (1) Dispensational concepts were taught by men who lived long before Darby. (2) It is to be expected that dispensationalism, which is so closely related to eschatology, would not be refined and systematized until recent times

[22]James Orr, *The Progress of Dogma* (Grand Rapids: Wm. B. Eerdmans Publishing Co.), pp. 24-30. Orr, a covenant theologian, has also written: "Existing systems are not final; as works of human understanding they are necessarily imperfect. . . . I do not question, therefore, that there are still sides and aspects of divine truth to which full justice has not yet been accorded; improvements that can be made in our conception and formulation of all the doctrines, and in their correlation with each other" (pp. 30-31).

simply because eschatology was not an area under discussion until then. The conclusions drawn from the charge of recency by opponents of dispensationalism are therefore unjustified. In all of this discussion, too, it is necessary to remember that the verdict of history is not the final authority. Every doctrine, whether ancient or recent, in the final analysis, must be tested by the light of the revelation of Scripture.

THE CHARGE OF DIVISIVENESS

Dispensationalism is not only charged with being recent but also with having originated in divisiveness. The inference is that anything that is factious in origin cannot be valid. Darby was a separatist; Plymouth Brethrenism is a separatist movement; and many adherents of dispensationalism today are found in movements which have separated from the larger denominations of Christendom; therefore, dispensationalism is a teaching which causes nothing but dissension in the church.

An example of this kind of attack is this:

> One need not scrutinize contemporary evangelical church life too closely to see this principle at work today. Nor does it take more than a casual survey of the history of theology since Darby's day to trace the continuity of his view of separation to our day. There exists a direct line from Darby through a number of channels—prophetic conferences, fundamentalistic movements, individual prophetic teachers, the Scofield Reference Bible, eschatological charts—all characterized by and contributing to a spirit of separatism and exclusion. The devastating effects of this spirit upon the total body of Christ cannot be underestimated.[23]

This kind of attack is based on two basic premises: (1) ecclesiastical separatism is always wrong, and (2) dispensationalism has been the principal (the inference is "only")

[23]Bass, *op. cit.*, p. 99.

factor causing ecclesiastical separation in the modern period. Both premises are fallacious.

Is ecclesiastical separation always wrong? Bass thinks that there is no question as to what the answer is. He declares *ex cathedra*: "Any theological system which causes a part of the church to withdraw from the larger fellowship in Christ and, by isolationism and separatism, to default its role, is wrong."[24] In similar vein Carnell says: "A spirit of divisiveness is not prompted by the Holy Spirit, for love is the law of life, and love remains unsatisfied until *all* who form the body of Christ are united in one sacred fellowship."[25]

To be sure, a party spirit is condemned in the Scriptures as carnality (I Cor. 3). But the same epistle declares that choices have to be made within ecclesiastical groups in order to mark off those who are approved (I Cor. 11:19). Schism and separatism are not synonymous concepts. One can be schismatic and still remain *within* a group, which does not make his schism right simply because he did not break away from that group. And one can be a separatist and break away from a group *and be right*. Whether or not organizational unity is maintained or broken is not the criterion for judging the rightness or wrongness of an action. To say that ecclesiastical separation is always wrong is not to think clearly about the Biblical concepts involved.

To say that ecclesiastical separatism is wrong is to condemn some of the most fruitful movements of church history. To try to classify the Reformation as "an eviction" in order not to have to classify it as a separatist movement is wishful thinking.[26] The plain, unvarnished fact is that Martin Luther broke with the Roman Catholic church and formed a new fellowship of believers. Therefore, he was a separatist, but he vigorously denied that he was a schismatic. A man can abhor

[24]*Ibid.*, p. 154.
[25]Carnell, *op. cit.*, p. 137.
[26]As Carnell does, *op. cit.*, pp. 136-37.

schism and be a separatist—as many of the reformers did and
were. If Bass' statement quoted above be true, then the theological system of the Reformation is wrong. There is no other
conclusion to be drawn, for there is no way to view the Reformation as anything but a separatist movement.

It is not necessary to speak of others like Thomas Chalmers,
Abraham Kuyper, or J. Gresham Machen, all of whom were
separatists but all of whom rejected the charge of being schis-
matics.[27] Were their actions wrong? Are the movements
which they initiated to be condemned? Was not the Holy
Spirit guiding them at all? If the reformers and others like
them were not guided by the Holy Spirit, then we had all
better make a contrite pilgrimage back to Rome and do it
quickly. But if any of these separatist movements were right
in their day, then conceivably separatist movements might be
right today.

The second premise underlying the charges against the
divisive nature of dispensationalism is that it alone or chiefly
has been the cause for divisions in the church. In none of
the examples just cited from history was dispensationalism a
factor in the separation. But, someone may say, those examples were not from the very modern period when dispensationalism had gained some prominence in theological discussion. This is true, but even in the contemporary scene dispensationalism has not been an issue at all in many of the
separatist movements. The American Council of Churches
and its worldwide affiliates are almost entirely nondispensational in theology. Indeed, they are covenant in their theological viewpoint. They could not possibly be charged even
with getting their doctrine of the apostate church from dis-

[27]Thomas Chalmers (1780-1847) in 1843 led about one third of the min-
isters of the Church of Scotland out of the General Assembly to organize the
Free Church of Scotland. Abraham Kuyper (1837-1920) withdrew from the
Dutch Reformed Church and founded in 1886 the Free Reformed Church.
J. Gresham Machen (1881-1937) left Princeton Theological Seminary because of modernism and founded Westminster Theological Seminary and
the independent board of missions.

pensationalism. The separatist Baptist groups did not originally separate from the larger denomination because of dispensationalism. The issue was modernism and the symptoms
of modernism were departures from very basic doctrines like
the virgin birth and the deity of Christ. Even in this present
hour the only separatist group which officially makes dispensationalism a part of its doctrinal basis is the Independent
Fundamental Churches of America (though modernism, not
dispensationalism, was originally the cause of the separation
of the churches in this fellowship). Contemporary church
history will not support the oft repeated statement or inference that dispensationalism has been the cause of ecclesiastical
separation.

Even in the first prophetic conference in this country in
1878 dispensationalism scarcely figured in the messages and
discussions.[28] Too, that conference and those that followed
were not convened because of a desire to promote dispensational truth. They grew as a protest to the rapid takeover of
existing denominations by modernism and the social gospel.
Inevitably, dispensationalism came into the messages of these
conferences, for the attention given to prophetic themes
focused men's minds on the literal interpretation of Scripture
and the distinction between Israel and the Church. But
there is little evidence that these men were borrowing from
Darby, and the Plymouth Brethren were not prominent in

[28]Even C. Norman Kraus admits this (*Dispensationalism in America*, p.
83). His attempt to link the prophetic conferences with dispensationalism is
in reverse gear. He tries to show that since there was some dispensational
teaching in the conferences this was the cause of their being convened.
The truth is that the calling of prophetic conferences as a protest to modernism was the cause, and a gradual understanding of dispensationalism was
the effect. The conferences led to dispensationalism, not vice versa. To be
sure there was an inevitable and eventual link between the conferences and
dispensationalism, but dispensationalism grew out of the *independent* study
which resulted from the interest in prophecy. Cf. also C. E. Harrington,
"The Fundamentalist Movement in America, 1870-1920" (unpublished Doctor's dissertation, University of California, 1959), and J. B. Behney, "Con-
servatism and Liberalism in the Late Nineteenth Century in American Protestantism" (unpublished Doctor's dissertation, Yale University, 1941).

the leadership of these conferences. The leaders were denominational men. The results of these early prophetic conferences were (1) an emphasis on literal interpretation of Scripture, (2) the imminency of the coming of Christ, (3) an emphasis on evangelism and missions, and (4) a firm stand against postmillennialism with its teaching of world conversion. Understanding of dispensationalism as it had been taught for fifty years by Darby before the first prophetic conference was only a by-product of the conferences and not an immediate one at that.

Notice should be taken also of the fact that the doctrine of the apostate church arose in these prophetic conferences as a reaction to postmillennialism's false optimism. Dispensationalism also taught the doctrine, but it originally entered the stream of American fundamentalism through the prophetic conferences more than through Darby. In any case, the doctrine of the apostate church was not the exclusive possession of dispensationalism. If this doctrine can be said to be "the most serious of all their [dispensationalists'] errors," then it could at one time have been said to be the most serious error of denominationalists too![29]

Modern opponents of dispensationalism have found it convenient to make dispensationalism the scapegoat and whipping boy for all the separatist movements in the church. This cannot be substantiated from history, and even if it were true, it would not necessarily be wrong. Separatism does not necessarily have to be schism whether it is caused by a desire for a pure doctrine of justification (as in the Reformation) or a pure doctrine of the church (as often in the modern era). After all, the Scriptures do teach an apostasy in the church during the last days which will lead to a great ecumenical superchurch (I Tim. 4:1-3; II Tim. 3:1-5; Rev. 17). Suppose dispensationalism had never developed beyond its unsystem-

[29]Norman C. Rhodes, *The Church Faces the Isms* (New York: Abingdon Press, 1958), p. 100.

atized form as existed before Darby, would this mean that there would have been no separatist movements in the recent history of the church? The answer is apparent.

In the light of the history of separatist movements it seems evident that the cause of separatism is deeper than any aspect or any one system of theology. Many factors have entered into each movement. Undoubtedly in no case could all the factors be justified. But underlying all these movements and coalescing all the factors is a common denominator, and that single factor, which is justifiable, is the desire to return to the Scriptures as the sole authority for faith and practice. This does not condone the surface dissension found in most separatist movements, particularly about the time of actual rupture, but it is to say that there is a proper and justifiable cause for separation. If in a larger segment of the church Bible truth or some aspect of it has been lost, and if within that segment a group attempts to emphasize that truth again, there is almost always bound to be a separation. Dispensationalism does foster Bible study, and if with that comes a dissatisfaction with an existing fellowship, it is not surprising. If Reformers feel that they can best serve the Lord outside the Roman church, or Scots outside the Church of Scotland, or Baptists outside the state church, or dispensationalists outside a denomination, is this necessarily wrong?

To sum up: Opponents of dispensationalism are quite inaccurate in bringing their charges that dispensationalism is recent and that it was born out of divisiveness. Dispensational concepts antedate Darby, although he played a large part in the systematizing and popularizing of dispensationalism. That such systematizing should occur late in the history of the church is to be expected in the chronological progress of doctrinal discussions. Although there were difficulties and factions *within* the early Brethren groups, the very first groups that met did not meet as a protest against anybody

CHART OF REPRESENTATIVE DISPENSATIONAL SCHEMES

PIERRE POIRET 1646-1719	JOHN EDWARDS 1639-1716	ISAAC WATTS 1674-1748	J. N. DARBY 1800-1882	JAMES H. BROOKES 1830-1897	JAMES M. GRAY 1851-1935 (Pub. 1901)	C. I. SCOFIELD 1843-1921 (Pub. 1909)
Creation to the Deluge (Infancy)	Innocency	Innocency	Paradisaical state (to the Flood)	Eden	Edenic	Innocency
	Adam fallen Antediluvian	Adamical (after the Fall)		Antediluvian	Antediluvian	Conscience
Deluge to Moses (Childhood)	Noahical	Noahical	Noah	Patriarchal	Patriarchal	Human Government
	Abrahamick	Abrahamical	Abraham			Promise
Moses to Prophets (Adolescence)	Mosaical	Mosaical	Israel— under law under priesthood under kings	Mosaic	Mosaic	Law
Prophets to Christ (Youth)						
Manhood and Old Age	Christian	Christian	Gentiles	Messianic	Church	Grace
			Spirit	Holy Ghost		
Renovation of All Things			Millennium	Millennial	Millennial	Kingdom
					Fullness of times	
					Eternal	

nor did they embark on an aggressive campaign against the Established Church. The lives of the men connected with any movement may credit or discredit its teachings, but they do not prove or disprove its truthfulness. Only the Bible does that.

One of the finest tributes to the beneficial effect of dispensationalism on American Christianity was paid by one whose own theology is nondispensational. Ladd has said:

> It is doubtful if there has been any other circle of men who have done more by their influence in preaching, teaching and writing to promote a love for Bible study, a hunger for the deeper Christian life, a passion for evangelism and zeal for missions in the history of American Christianity.[30]

This is high praise for any system of theology.

[30]Ladd, *op. cit.*, p. 49.

5

THE HERMENEUTICS OF DISPENSATIONALISM

HERMENEUTICS is that science which furnishes the principles of interpretation. These principles guide and govern anybody's system of theology. They ought to be determined *before* one's theology is systematized, but in practice the reverse is usually true. At least in the awareness of most people, hermeneutics is one of the last things to be considered consciously. Most people know something of the doctrines they believe, but little of the hermeneutics on which they have been built. Principles of interpretation are basic and ought to be established before attempting to interpret the Word so that the result is not only right interpretation but a right system of theology.

THE OPPOSING VIEWPOINTS

A. THE DISPENSATIONALIST'S POSITION

Dispensationalists claim that their principle of hermeneutics is that of literal interpretation. This means interpretation which gives to every word the same meaning it would have in normal usage, whether employed in writing, speaking or thinking.[1] This is sometimes called the principle of grammatical-historical interpretation since the meaning of each

[1]Bernard Ramm, *Protestant Biblical Interpretation* (Boston: W. A. Wilde, 1956), pp. 89-92.

word is determined by grammatical and historical considerations. The principle might also be called normal interpretation since the literal meaning of words is the normal approach to their understanding in all languages. It might also be designated plain interpretation so that no one receives the mistaken notion that the literal principle rules out figures of speech. Symbols, figures of speech and types are all interpreted plainly in this method and they are in no way contrary to literal interpretation. After all, the very existence of any meaning for a figure of speech depends on the reality of the literal meaning of the terms involved. Figures often make the meaning plainer, but it is the literal, normal, or plain meaning that they convey to the reader. "The *literalist* (so called) is not one who denies that *figurative* language, that *symbols*, are used in prophecy, nor does he deny that great *spiritual* truths are set forth therein; his position is, simply, that the prophecies are to be *normally* interpreted (i.e., according to the received laws of language) as any other utterances are interpreted—that which is manifestly figurative being so regarded."[2]

There are many reasons given by dispensationalists to support this hermeneutical principle of literal, normal, or plain interpretation. At least three are worthy of mention at this point.

Philosophically, the purpose of language itself seems to require literal interpretation. Language was given by God for the purpose of being able to communicate with man. As Clark says:

> If God created man in His own rational image and endowed him with the power of speech, then a purpose of language, in fact the chief purpose of language, would naturally be the revelation of truth to man and the prayers of man to God. In a theistic philosophy one

[2]J. P. Lange, *Commentary on the Holy Scriptures: Revelation* (New York: Charles Scribner, 1872), p. 98.

ought not to say that all language has been devised in order to describe and discuss the finite objects of our sense-experience. . . . On the contrary, language was devised by God, that is, God created man rational for the purpose of theological expression.[3]

If God be the originator of language and if the chief purpose of originating it was to convey His message to man, then it must follow that He, being all-wise and all-loving, originated sufficient language to convey all that was in His heart to tell man. Furthermore, it must also follow that He would use language and expect man to use it in its literal, normal, and plain sense. The Scriptures, then, cannot be regarded as an illustration of some special use of language so that in the interpretation of these Scriptures some deeper meaning of the words must be sought. If language is the creation of God for the purpose of conveying His message, then a theist must view that language as sufficient in scope and normative in use in accomplishing that purpose for which God originated it.

A second reason why dispensationalists believe in the literal principle is a Biblical one. It is simply this: the prophecies in the Old Testament concerning the first coming of Christ—His birth, His rearing, His ministry, His death, His resurrection—were all fulfilled literally. There is no nonliteral fulfillment of these prophecies in the New Testament. This argues strongly for the literal method.

A third reason is a logical one. If one does not use the plain, normal, or literal method of interpretation, all objectivity is lost. What check would there be on the variety of interpretations which man's imagination could produce if there were not an objective standard which the literal principle provides? To try to see meaning other than the normal

[3]Gordon Clark, "Special Divine Revelation as Rational," *Revelation and the Bible*, ed. by C. F. H. Henry (Grand Rapids: Baker Book House, 1958), p. 41.

one would result in as many interpretations as there are people interpreting. Literalism is a logical rationale.

Of course, literal interpretation is not the exclusive property of dispensationalists. Most conservatives would agree with what has just been said. What, then, is the difference between the dispensationalists' use of this hermeneutical principle and the nondispensationalists'? The difference lies in the fact that the dispensationalist claims to use the normal principle of interpretation *consistently* in *all* his study of the Bible. He further claims that the nondispensationalist does not use the principle everywhere. He admits that the nondispensationalist is a literalist in much of his interpretation of the Scriptures, but charges him with allegorizing or spiritualizing when it comes to the interpretation of prophecy. The dispensationalist claims to be consistent in his use of this principle, and he accuses the nondispensationalist of being inconsistent in his use of it.

Notice, for instance, the predicament one recent writer gets himself into by not using the literal principle consistently.[4] He recognizes that some insist on a literal fulfillment of prophecy while others see only a symbolic meaning. His suggestion is that prophecy should be approached *"in terms of equivalents, analogy, or correspondence."*[5] As an example of the application of this principle he mentions the weapons cited in Ezekiel 39, and states that these will not be the exact weapons used in the future war; rather equivalent weapons will be used. But suppose this principle of equivalents were applied to Micah 5: 2. Then any small town in Palestine in which Christ would have been born would have satisfactorily fulfilled the prophecy. If the Bible says "like chariots" or "like Bethlehem," then there may be some latitude in interpretation. But if specific details are not interpreted literally when given as

[4]A. Berkeley Mickelsen, *Interpreting the Bible* (Grand Rapids: Wm. B. Eerdmans Publishing Co., 1963), pp. 296-305.
[5]*Ibid.*, p. 296.

specific details, then there can be no end to the variety of meanings of a text.

B. THE NONDISPENSATIONALIST'S POSITION

Perhaps this distinction between the two viewpoints can be best seen by noting what the nondispensationalist has to say about this matter of hermeneutics, especially as it relates to the application of the principle of literal interpretation to prophecy. For instance, Allis, a champion of covenant theology and amillennialism and a vigorous opponent of dispensationalism, says:

> One of the most marked features of premillennialism in all its forms is the emphasis which it places on the literal interpretation of Scripture. It is the insistent claims of its advocates that only when interpreted literally is the Bible interpreted truly; and they denounce as "spiritualizers" or "allegorizers" those who do not interpret the Bible with the same degree of literalness as they do. None have made this charge more pointedly than the dispensationalists.[6]

In his words, the issue between dispensationalists and nondispensationalists is "the same degree of literalness." More specifically this has to do with the interpretation of prophecy. The dispensationalist claims to apply his literal principle to all Scripture, including prophecy, while the nondispensationalist does not apply it to prophecy. He does apply it to other areas of truth, and this is evident from the simple fact that there is no disagreement with dispensationalists over these doctrines. But that he does not apply it to prophecy is also evident, for if he did he would not arrive at amillennialism. Allis himself admits that "the Old Testament prophecies if literally interpreted cannot be regarded as having been yet

[6]Oswald T. Allis, *Prophecy and the Church* (Philadelphia: Presbyterian and Reformed Publishing Co., 1945), p. 17.

fulfilled or as being capable of fulfillment in this present age."[7]

Of course there are nondispensational premillennialists. But these men, like the amillennialist, do not apply the literal principle consistently. They apply it more extensively than the amillennialist but not so extensively as the dispensationalist.[8] In other words, the nondispensationalist position is simply that the literal principle is sufficient except for the interpretation of prophecy. In this area, the spiritualizing principle of interpretation must be introduced. The amillennialist uses it in the entire area of prophetic truth; the covenant premillennialist uses it only partially. This is why the dispensationalist claims he is the only one who uses literalism consistently.

Many years ago Peters warned of the dangers of spiritualizing of any sort in interpreting the Scriptures. His words are still appropriate:

> The prophecies referring to the Kingdom of God, as now interpreted by the large majority of Christians, afford the strongest leverage employed by unbelievers against Christianity. Unfortunately, unbelief is often logically correct. Thus, e.g., it eagerly points to the predictions pertaining to David's Son, showing that, if language has any *legitimate* meaning, and words are *adequate* to express an idea, they *unmistakably* predict the restoration of David's throne and kingdom, etc., and then triumphantly declare that it was not realized (so Strauss, Baur, Renan, Parker, etc.). They mock the expectation of the Jews, of Simeon, the preaching of John, Jesus, and the disciples, the anticipations of the early Church, and hastily conclude, sustained by *the present*

[7]*Ibid.*, p. 238.
[8]Cf. the interpretation of the 144,000 in George E. Ladd, *The Blessed Hope* (Grand Rapids: Wm. B. Eerdmans Publishing Co., 1956), p. 126, and J. Barton Payne, *The Imminent Appearing of Christ* (Grand Rapids: Wm. B. Eerdmans Publishing Co., 1962), p. 63. Literalism would end their uncertainty in interpretation of this point!

faith of the Church (excepting only a few), that *they will never be* fulfilled; and that, therefore, the prophecies, the foundation upon which the superstructure rests, are false, and of human concoction. The manner of meeting such objections is *humiliating* to the Word and Reason; for it discards *the plain grammatical sense* as unreliable, and, to save the credit of the Word, insists upon interpreting all such prophecies by adding to them under the claim of spiritual, a sense which *is not contained in the language,* but suits the religious system adopted. Unbelief is not slow in seizing *the advantage* thus given, gleefully pointing out how this introduced change makes the ancient faith an ignorant one, the early Church occupying a false position, and the Bible a book to which man adds any sense, under the plea of spiritual, that may be deemed necessary for its defense.[9]

THE IMPORTANCE OF CONSISTENCY

Theoretically at least, the application of the literal principle is not debated. Most agree that this involves some obvious procedures. For one thing, the meaning of each word must be studied. This involves etymology, use, history, and resultant meaning. For another thing, the grammar or relationship of the words to each other must be analyzed. For a third thing, the context, immediate and remote, must be considered. This means comparing scripture with scripture as well as the study of the immediate context. These principles are well known and can be studied in any standard text on hermeneutics.

However, in practice the theory is often compromised or adjusted and in effect vitiated. The amillennialist does this in his entire approach to eschatology. This has already been

[9]George N. H. Peters, *The Theocratic Kingdom* (Grand Rapids: Kregel Publications, 1952), I, 167-68 . This quotation is not to suggest that amillennialists are in the same category as unbelievers. They are not, for they are conservative in other areas of theology. But the quotation does show in a very striking way the dangers of anything but consistently literal interpretation.

mentioned. Hamilton, for instance, who is an amillennialist, confessed:

> Now we must frankly admit that a literal interpretation
> of the Old Testament prophecies gives us just such a pic-
> ture of an earthly reign of the Messiah as the premillen-
> nialist pictures. That was the kind of Messianic king-
> dom that the Jews of the time of Christ were looking for,
> on the basis of a literal kingdom interpretation of the
> Old Testament promises.[10]

But, having confessed this, he then arrives at a different picture of the kingdom and on the basis of different herme- neutics. He feels, of course, that he has found justifiable reasons for spiritualizing the concept of the kingdom, but the important point is that his resultant picture stems from a principle of hermeneutics which is not literal (for if he fol- lowed the literal principle he admits, he would be a pre- millennialist). The change from a literal procedure is not difficult to see in amillennialism.

The premillennialist who is antidispensational also com- promises the literal principle. This is done by what Fuller, a recent representative of this group, calls theological interpreta- tion. He explains:

> In Covenant Theology there is the tendency to impute
> to passages a meaning which would not be gained merely
> from their historical and grammatical associations. This
> phase of interpretation is called the "theological" inter-
> pretation.[11]

This is quite an admission, for it means that the covenant premillennialist is not a consistent literalist by his own state- ment. If he were, he would have to be a dispensationalist, and he seems to know it! An example of this hybrid literal-theo-

[10]Floyd E. Hamilton, *The Basis of Millennial Faith* (Grand Rapids: Wm. B. Eerdmans Publishing Co., 1942), p. 38.
[11]Daniel P. Fuller, "The Hermeneutics of Dispensationalism" (Doctor's dis- sertation, Northern Baptist Theological Seminary, Chicago, 1957), p. 147.

logical principle in action is given by Fuller in connection
with the promises made to Abraham. He states (correctly)
that the dispensationalist understands the promises to require
two seeds, a physical and a spiritual seed for Abraham. He
notes that the amillennialist "depreciates the physical aspect of
the seed of Abraham so much that the promises made to Abraham's physical seed no longer mean what they say, but are
interpreted strictly in spiritual terms. This mediating position [that of the covenant premillennialist] still asserts that a
literalistic procedure, which also interprets theologically by
regarding progressive revelation, is the basic hermeneutical
approach."[12]

Thus the nondispensationalist is not a consistent literalist
by his own admission, but has to introduce another hermeneutical principle (the "theological" method) in order to
have a hermeneutical basis for the system which he holds.
One suspects that the conclusions determined the means used
to arrive at them—which is a charge usually hurled at dispensationalists!

Fuller's problem is that apparently his concept of progressive revelation includes the possibility that subsequent revelation may completely change the meaning of something previously revealed. It is true that progressive revelation brings
additional light, but does it completely reverse to the point
of contradiction what has been previously revealed? Fuller's
concept apparently allows for such, but the literal principle
built upon a sound philosophy of the purpose of language
does not. New revelation cannot mean contradictory revelation. Later revelation on a subject does not make the earlier
revelation mean something different. It may add to it or
even supersede it, but it does not contradict it. A word or
concept cannot mean one thing in the Old Testament and
take on opposite meaning in the New Testament. If this were
so, then the Bible would be filled with contradictions, and

[12]*Ibid.*, p. 238.

does not use consistently the literal principle which he believes in sees some of them fulfilled literally and some not. Fuller makes a startling confession when he says that "the whole problem of how far a literal interpretation of the Old Testament prophets is to be carried is still very perplexing to the present writer."[15] The admission is even the more surprising when one realizes that it is made in the last paragraph of his chapter on conclusions. The consistent application of literal interpretation would solve his problem, for the Scriptures would speak to him as they did to the prophets, plainly and at face value.

Since literal interpretation results in taking the Scriptures at face value, it also results in recognizing distinctions in the Scriptures. No interpreter of Scripture denies this fact, but the extent to which he recognizes distinctions is the evidence of his consistent use of the literal principle of interpretation. It is not a matter of superimposing a dual purpose of God on the Scriptures, but it is a matter of recognizing that in the New Testament the word *Israel* does not mean the Church and vice versa. The dispensationalist, then, recognizes the different peoples of God simply because of the distinction maintained by the text as literally interpreted.

Taking the text at face value and recognizing distinctions in the process of revelation leads to the recognition of differing economies in the outworking of God's program. In other words, consistent literalism is the basis for dispensationalism, and since consistent literalism is the logical and obvious principle of interpretation, dispensationalism is more than justified. It is only by adjusting or adding to the principle of literal interpretation that dispensationalism is avoided. Face-value understanding incorporates distinctions; distinctions lead to dispensations. Normal interpretation leads to the clear distinction between words, concepts, peoples, and

[15]Fuller, *op. cit.*, p. 374.

economies. This consistent hermeneutical principle is the
basis of dispensationalism.

THE UNIFYING PRINCIPLE OF THE BIBLE

The distinctions resulting from the application of the
literal principle have brought the charge that dispensationalism destroys the unity of the Bible. From the more scholarly opponents of dispensationalism the charges run like this:
Dispensationalism "is therefore unable to display the unity of
the Bible . . ."[16] or ". . . the Bible ceases to be a self-consistent
whole."[17]

> More popularly the charge is expressed in words like these:
> [Satan] advanced a much more modified form of dispen-
> sationalism—a form so mild and so moderate that by the
> great majority of fundamentalists it was accepted. In
> fact, fundamentalism and *mild dispensationalism* are
> today almost synonymous. Yet in its tendencies, funda-
> mentalist dispensationalism is, we believe, dangerous
> and mischievous, robbing us of much of the Bible, espe-
> cially of the words of Christ.[18]

In the same chapter from which this quotation was taken
(which incidentally is entitled "Have You Lost Your
Bible?") the author names destructive higher criticism as
another example of Satan's efforts to rob people of parts of
the Bible. This is another example of an unfair method of
attacking dispensationalism—the use of the guilt-by-association tactic. Surprisingly this unworthy tactic is used by no
less a scholar and gentleman than Allis, who makes the same
comparison between dispensationalism and higher criticism:

> Dispensationalism shares with higher criticism its funda-
> mental error. . . . In a word, despite all their differences,

[16]*Ibid.,* p. 371.
[17]Oswald T. Allis, "Modern Dispensationalism and the Law of God," *The
Evangelical Quarterly,* 8 (July 15, 1936), 872.
[18]T. A. Hegre, *The Cross and Sanctification* (Minneapolis: Bethany Fellowship, 1960), pp. 3-4.

> higher criticism and dispensationalism are in this one respect strikingly similar. Higher criticism divides the Scriptures up into documents which differ from or contradict one another. Dispensationalists divide the Bible up into dispensations which differ from and even contradict one another [19]

It is scarcely necessary to say how unjust such a comparison is. But the charge, however stated, boils down to an accusation that dispensationalism so compartmentalizes the Bible that its unity is completely destroyed.

Undoubtedly dispensationalists have given the impression that the dispensations are so many compartments, like separate post office boxes, which have no connection with each other. But dispensationalists have also had much to say about the unity of the Bible, and there is no excuse for nondispensationalists recognizing only one side of what dispensationalists say, unless that be an easier straw man to attack! Fuller, his protests notwithstanding, has set up a straw man in what he calls "normative dispensationalism," which is what he thinks dispensationalism logically ought to be—whether it is or not. These opponents are slow to recognize any refinements in dispensational teaching and quick to allow for them in their own.[20] For all that they did accomplish, Darby, Scofield, and Chafer cannot be expected to have said everything that could be said about dispensationalism in their lifetimes. Dispensationalists have emphasized the unity of the Scriptures whether the nondispensationalist wishes to acknowledge it or not.

As an example, let us note what one "normative dispensationalist" says about the unity of Scripture. Scofield, who does not have one word to say about dispensations in his in-

[19]Oswald T. Allis, "Modern Dispensationalism and the Doctrine of the Unity of the Scriptures," *The Evangelical Quarterly*, 8 (January, 1936), 24.
[20]Fuller, *op. cit.*, pp. 199-203; cf. p. 374, where the author expresses the hope that future study will help clarify some of the perplexities in his own system.

troduction to the Reference Bible (which Introduction is
specifically designated *"TO BE READ"*), does have quite
a bit to say about the unity of the Bible:

> *First, The Bible is one book.* Seven great marks attest
> this unity. (1) From Genesis the Bible bears witness to
> *one God.* . . . (2) The Bible forms one *continuous
> story.* . . . (3) The Bible hazards the most unlikely
> *predictions* concerning the future. . . . (4) The Bible is
> a *progressive* unfolding of truth. . . . (5) From begin-
> ning to end the Bible testifies to *one redemption.* (6)
> From beginning to end the Bible has *one great theme—*
> the person and work of the Christ. (7) And, finally,
> these writers, some forty-four in number, writing
> through twenty centuries, have produced a *perfect har-
> mony* of doctrine in progressive unfolding.[21]

Other dispensationalists, like Erich Sauer and W. Graham
Scroggie (*The Unfolding Drama of Redemption*), give strong
emphasis to the unity of the Bible and prominence to God's
redemptive purpose.

Unity and distinction are not necessarily contradictory
concepts. Examples abound. The human body is not dis-
united because the hand is distinct from the ear. The unity
of a building is not impaired by carefully observing the
distinctions between the iron and wood that go into it.
Furthermore, in the process of building, each part must wait
its proper time and order of entering into the overall development. Or "the unity of a touchdown by a football team is not
destroyed by the making of several separate and distinguishable first downs by different methods during the connected
march toward the goal line."[22] Even in areas of theology
which nondispensationalists do not dispute with dispensationalists they recognize that distinctions do not necessarily

[21]The Scofield Reference Bible, p. v.
[22]James E. Rosscup, "Crucial Objections to Dispensationalism" (unpublished Master's thesis, Dallas Theological Seminary, 1961), p. 74.

mean disunity. "The unity of the Trinity is most certainly admitted by conservative opponents of dispensationalism; yet these theologians are very careful to maintain distinctions in the three Persons comprising the Godhead! This unity with distinctions is recognized also in the doctrine of the hypostatic union of the two natures in the one Person of the incarnate Christ!"[23] Even the nondispensationalist does not consider the unity of his sermon destroyed by the compartments of its divisions. "Sameness does not always produce unity nor differences disunity. A more impossible situation could not be imagined than a jigsaw puzzle composed wholly of circles."[24] Unity and distinction are not necessarily incompatible concepts. They may be quite complementary, as indeed they are in dispensationalism.

Even though dispensationalists do speak of the unity of the Bible, and even though nondispensationalists fail to recognize that distinctions may be involved in unity, the charge that dispensationalism destroys the unity of the Bible still persists. What is this unity which is supposedly destroyed? It is, in the nondispensationalists' opinion, the unity of the overall purpose of redemption. The so-called covenant of grace is the governing category by which all Scripture is to be understood. God's purpose in the world is to redeem, and men have been, are, and will always be redeemed in the same manner throughout all time. Any distinctions which are recognized by the covenant theologian are merely aspects of the outworking of this single purpose as controlled by the covenant of grace. "Everything in history and life is subservient to spiritual redemption," says one covenant writer.[25] More recently Bass, an opponent of dispensationalism, states that "the church, as the body of Christ providentially redeemed,

[23]*Ibid.*
[24]H. Chester Woodring, "Grace Under the Mosaic Covenant" (unpublished Doctor's dissertation, Dallas Theological Seminary, 1956), p. 28.
[25]Roderick Campbell, *Israel and the New Covenant* (Philadelphia: Presbyterian Board of Christian Education, 1936), p. 14.

is the epitome of the whole structure of God's purposes on the earth."[26] Fuller states it equally plainly when he says:

> There are those, on the one hand, who see the Bible as the outworking of God's one purpose of redemption, whose focal point is in the cross of Christ. This is the traditional view voiced by the conservative elements within the major denominational groups.[27]

No dispensationalist minimizes the importance of God's saving purpose in the world. But whether it is God's total purpose or even His principal purpose is open to question. The dispensationalist sees a broader purpose in God's program for the world than salvation, and that purpose is His own glory. For the dispensationalist the glory of God is the governing principle and overall purpose, and the soteriological program is one of the principal means employed in bringing to pass the greatest demonstration of His own glory. Salvation is part and parcel of God's program, but it cannot be equated with the entire purpose itself. John F. Walvoord, president of Dallas Theological Seminary, has stated this quite clearly:

> All the events of the created world are designed to manifest the glory of God. The error of covenant theologians is that they combine all the many facets of divine purpose in the one objective of the fulfillment of the covenant of grace. From a logical standpoint this is the reductive error—the use of one aspect of the whole as the determining element.[28]

Thus, as stated in chapter 1, the unifying principle of covenant theology is in practice, soteriological. The unifying principle of dispensationalism is doxological, or the glory of God, and the dispensations reveal the glory of God as He

[26]C. B. Bass, *Backgrounds to Dispensationalism* (Grand Rapids: Wm. B. Eerdmans Publishing Co., 1960), p. 9.
[27]Fuller, *op. cit.*, p. 6.
[28]John F. Walvoord, *The Millennial Kingdom* (Findlay, Ohio: Dunham Publishing Co., 1959), p. 92.

manifests His character in the differing stewardships given to man.

But, someone may object, is this in reality not simply a minor distinction? Are not the glory of God and the saving work of God practically the same concept? Not at all. The glory of God is manifesting God for who He is. God as a consuming fire (Heb. 12:29) reveals the judicial side of God's character, and it is not a display of redemption. Without getting involved with all the questions concerning salvation under the period of the Mosaic Law, it is quite clear that God had some purpose under the Law beside the soteriological. Otherwise, how can we take at face value Paul's statement that the law was "the ministration of death" and "the ministration of condemnation" (II Cor. 3:7, 9)? These are not descriptions of salvation to say the least!

How do we know that the glory of God is the purpose of God above and beyond His saving purpose? First, the plain statement of Scripture declares that salvation is to the praise of God's glory which simply means that redemption is one of the means to the end of glorifying God (Eph. 1:6, 12, 14). Salvation, for all of its wonder, is but one facet of the diamond of the glory of God. Second, all theologians of whatever persuasion realize that God has a plan for the angels. It does not involve redemption, for the elect angels do not experience it and the nonelect angels cannot. And yet for the angels God has a distinct program—a distinct purpose, and it is not soteriological. Third, if one is a premillennialist (not even necessarily of the dispensational variety) he recognizes that in the kingdom program God has a purpose which, though it involves salvation, is not confined to redemption. Obviously God has other purposes in this world besides the redemption of mankind, though with our man-centered perspective we are prone to forget that fact.

It is recognized that the covenant theologian declares that

the glory of God is the chief purpose of God. For instance, Hodge says that "the final cause of all God's purposes is His own glory."[29] Shedd is more specific: "Neither salvation nor damnation are ultimate ends, but means to an ultimate end: namely, the manifested glory of the Triune God."[30] But covenant theology makes *the* means of manifesting the glory of God the plan of redemption. Thus, for all practical purposes, covenant theology uses redemption as its unifying principle. This is undoubtedly partly due to the spiritualizing of the text of Scripture so that there is little or no future for Israel, thus obliterating the distinctive purpose God has for that people. If that were not obliterated, then the covenant theologian would see that the glory of God is to be realized fully not only in salvation but also in the Jewish people and also in His purpose concerning angels.

God does have various ways to manifest His glory, redemption being one—a principal one, but not the only one. The various economies with their stewardship responsibilities are not so many compartments completely separated from each other but are stages in the progress of the revelation of the various ways in which God is glorified. And further, dispensationalism not only sees the various dispensations as *successive* manifestations of God's purpose but also as *progressive* manifestations of it. The entire program culminates, not in eternity but in history, in the millennial kingdom of the Lord Christ. This millennial culmination is the climax of history and the great goal of God's program for the ages.

> In accord with the general thesis of Biblical theism, the achievement of this goal in the historical process is effected only by divine aid, for fallen man is helpless in the conflict of good and evil apart from the grace of

[29]Charles Hodge, *Systematic Theology* (Grand Rapids: Wm. B. Eerdmans Publishing Co., 1940), I, 535.
[30]William G. T. Shedd, *Dogmatic Theology* (New York: Scribner's, 1889), I, 448.

God. A unique feature of dispensationalism is that this conflict does not assume a more or less fixed pitch. Rather it rises in a mighty crescendo, as in ever new forms by historical and experimental proof is demonstrated through respective dispensations man's supreme need of grace to attain to the glory of God.[31]

Dispensationalism alone sees the unity, the variety, and the progressiveness of this purpose of God for the world.

ADDITIONAL NOTE ON THE SERMON ON THE MOUNT

In relation to the matter of interpretation, one of the favorite targets for the attack of opponents of dispensationalism is what they consider to be the dispensationalists' view of the Sermon on the Mount. The dispensationalists' position concerning its teachings is alleged to be that "the requirements of the Sermon are irrelevant for this age and legalistic . . ."[32] Another critic asserts that dispensationalists teach "that the Sermon on the Mount is neither the Church's duty nor privilege. It is not for now."[33] Kraus echoes the "party line" and misrepresents dispensationalism by insisting that in it "Jesus' life and teachings are lost to the Church."[34]

The picture of dispensational teaching given the Christian public is that of a knife which not only makes hairsplitting distinctions but actually cuts away parts of the Bible. On the basis of this picture Christians are urged to reject dispensationalism. Or, as Ladd puts it: "A system which takes this great portion of Jesus' teaching away from the Christian in its direct application must receive penetrating scrutiny."[35]

[31]Woodring, *op. cit.*, p. 42.
[32]C. F. H. Henry, *Christian Personal Ethics* (Grand Rapids: Wm. B. Eerdmans Publishing Co., 1957), p. 292.
[33]Hegre, *op. cit.*, p. 6.
[34]C. Norman Kraus, *Dispensationalism in America* (Richmond: John Knox Press, 1958), p. 133.
[35]G. E. Ladd, *Crucial Questions About the Kingdom of God* (Grand Rapids: Wm. B. Eerdmans Publishing Co., 1952), p. 104.

Why is the Sermon on the Mount made the focus of the attack? Nobody ever criticizes dispensationalism for teaching that the dietary regulations of the Mosaic law have no application to the Christian. The Sermon on the Mount, however, is different. It contains the Golden Rule, the Lord's Prayer, and other favorite passages. To suggest even that its direct relation to the Christian is open to question inevitably involves people's emotions before their doctrine. Of course the dietary laws are just as much inspired Scripture as the Sermon on the Mount—a fact which emotions easily overlook.

No matter who views the Sermon on the Mount, he has to make some "adjustments" in its statements. The humanist repudiates its teachings entirely. The theological liberal sees it as Jesus' showing us the way in which to walk, but complete conformity is impossible if the commands are taken literally.[36] The nondispensational conservative views the Sermon as the expression of "the only righteousness acceptable to God in this age or in any.[37] But in interpreting the Sermon's righteousness, even the conservative is required to abandon literal interpretation if he attempts to make it directly applicable to the believer today. For instance, Ladd, who also believes the Sermon is the standard of righteousness for this age, more than once inveighs against understanding the Sermon with "wooden literalness." He cites as his proof the fact that even Jesus did not turn the other cheek (John 18:23) ; therefore, we need not understand these words with "wooden literalness."[38] The obvious question that arises from such fudging or "adjusting" of the text is, If you abandon literal interpretation, whose understanding of the "underlying meaning" is correct? But if the laws of the Sermon are to be obeyed today they could not be taken literally, for, as Ladd points out,

[36]Major, Manson, and Wright, *The Mission and Message of Jesus* (London: Ivor Nicholson and Watson, 1937), p. 470.
[37]Henry, *op. cit.*, p. 308.
[38]George E. Ladd, *The Gospel of the Kingdom* (Grand Rapids: Wm. B. Eerdmans Publishing Co., 1959), p. 88.

every businessman would go bankrupt giving to those who ask of him. This is the dilemma every interpreter faces. If literal, it cannot be for today; if for today, it cannot be literal. And this is not a dilemma that faces only dispensationalists.

The point is perfectly plain: Whatever the dispensational interpreter may do to the Sermon, it might not be as bad as the nondispensationalist's adjusting and spiritualizing. Indeed, it can be said that even the nondispensationalist does not apply the Sermon fully today, even though he tries to apply it directly.

Now, what does dispensationalism say about the Sermon? It says two things: (1) The Sermon is primarily related to the Messianic kingdom. (2) Like all Scripture, the Sermon is applicable to believers in this age. It is only the first of these two that opponents of dispensationalism mention, but the application of the Sermon to believers now is also clearly taught by dispensationalists. Chafer, who is often quoted on the kingdom relevance of the Sermon, says on the same page from which the kingdom application is quoted: "A secondary application to the church means that lessons and principles may be drawn from it."[39] This is exactly what the nondispensationalist says with the exception of the word "secondary." He also is forced to use the word "principles" in speaking of what in the Sermon is to be obeyed by the church simply because the literal obedience to the laws is impossible today.[40]

The dispensationalist does recognize the relevance and application of the teachings of the Sermon to believers today regardless of how much nondispensationalists want to make him say otherwise.[41] The dispensationalist, however, views the primary fulfillment of the Sermon and the full following

[39]L. S. Chafer, *Systematic Theology* (Dallas: Seminary Press, 1947), V, 97.
[40]Ladd, *The Gospel of the Kingdom*, p. 88: ". . . principles which have never been abrogated."
[41]Cf. the author's *Biblical Theology of the New Testament* (Chicago: Moody Press, 1959), pp. 81-82.

of its laws as applicable to the Messianic kingdom. After all, there are many other passages of Scripture which all conservative interpreters recognize are not primarily applicable to believers today but which have secondary relevance today in the principles they set forth. Dispensationalists believe that anger, lust, divorce, and murder are sin, and they believe it on the basis of the Sermon on the Mount. Dispensationalists believe that the Golden Rule and the Lord's Prayer are excellent guides. But they also believe that the full, nonfudging, unadjusted fulfillment of the Sermon relates to the kingdom of Messiah, and at the same time they do not postpone the relevance of the Sermon to a future age.[42]

This is the heart of the dispensationalist's interpretation of the Sermon. Is it so bad? At least it does justice to literal interpretation, and the consistency of one's hermeneutical principle is far more important than the defense of one's theological system. It in no way disregards the importance of the ethical teachings of the Sermon for today, and it gives proper recognition to the ultimate purpose of the Sermon.

A few minor matters remain. One is this: It is usually charged that dispensationalists teach that the Sermon is all law and no gospel.[43] To those who object to this claim, we merely ask, Where can one find a statement of the gospel in the Sermon? The best Henry can do to answer that question is this: "The standpoint of grace dominates the whole biblical revelation after the fall."[44] But a plain statement of the gospel neither he nor anyone else can find in the Sermon.

Another matter is this: Dispensationalists often point out the absence from the Sermon of Church truth. It is readily admitted that this does not prove that the Sermon is not primarily for the Church, but it is very strange that this most

---

[42]As Henry alleges in a typical nondispensationalist's overstatement of the dispensational viewpoint (*op. cit.*, p. 292).

[43]Henry, *op. cit.*, p. 287.

[44]*Ibid.*, p. 290.

complete of all the teachings of Jesus does not mention the Holy Spirit once, or the Church per se, or prayer in the name of Christ. These things were taught by Christ on other occasions during His ministry but not in the Sermon (cf. John 14:16; 16:13, 24; Matt. 16:18). Concerning prayer, the Lord said later that it was to be offered in His name—a rather important fact which the Sermon nowhere reveals. This is a serious omission from that which is "the rule of *daily* life for the *Christian* believer."[45] The usual nondispensationalist reply to these assertions is that the Sermon must be supplemented by the teaching of the remainder of the New Testament. But such supplementation appears to involve some major differences which makes one suspicious of any interpretation that sets forth the Sermon as the believer's rule of life.

Thus the dispensational interpretation of the Sermon on the Mount simply tries to follow consistently the principle of literal, normal, or plain interpretation. It results in not trying to relegate primarily and fully the teachings of the Sermon to the believer in this age. But it does not in the least disregard the ethical principles of the Sermon as being not only applicable but also binding on believers today. Can this be called "cutting out pages from the Bible"?

[45]*Ibid.*, p. 308 (italics in quotation mine).

6

SALVATION IN DISPENSATIONALISM

WITHOUT DOUBT the most frequently heard objection against dispensationalism is that it is supposed to teach several ways of salvation. In particular, dispensationalists are said to teach salvation by works in some dispensations and salvation by grace in others. This is a very serious charge and therefore must be examined with extreme care.

THE CHARGE

A. STATEMENT OF THE CHARGE

The charge that dispensationalism teaches multiple ways of salvation is repeated with the regularity of a dripping faucet. Bowman declared in 1956:

> . . . If any man is saved in any dispensation other than those of Promise and Grace, he is saved by *works* and not by faith! [The dispensationalist] is clearly left with two methods of salvation on his hands—*works* for the majority of dispensations, *faith* for the rest—and we have . . . to deal with a fickle God who deals with man in various ways at various times.[1]

In 1960 Bass put similar words into the mouths of dispensationalists by concluding that:

[1]John Wick Bowman, "The Bible and Modern Religions: II, Dispensationalism," *Interpretation,* 10 (April, 1956), 178.

> . . . the presupposition of the difference between law and grace, between Israel and the Church, between the different relations of God to men in the different dispensations, when carried to its logical conclusion, will inevitably result in a multiple form of salvation—that men are not saved the same way in all ages.[2]

In 1957 Fuller acknowledged in his dissertation that dispensationalists deny this charge. He called this the "new emphasis in dispensationalism," and described it as unwillingness to follow the logic that led Chafer and Scofield to teach, so he says, two ways of salvation. It seems more like the logic which nondispensationalists have tried to force on dispensationalists, for even these men, who constitute the "old emphasis in dispensationalism," did not teach what they are charged with. Nevertheless, the attack persists despite repeated denials on the part of dispensationalists. One almost gathers that antidispensationalists do not want to hear what is being said since it is more convenient to attack the so-called logical conclusions forced on dispensationalism.

B. REASONS FOR THE CHARGE

There are undoubtedly reasons—whether justified or not— why the attack persists. For one thing, the labeling of the present dispensation as that of Grace has been taken to mean dispensationalism teaches there was no grace in any other age. Antidispensationalists will not even allow the dispensationalist to speak of less or more grace in various dispensations; it has to be an all or none proposition. So Fuller sweepingly concludes: "Hence it is impossible to think of varying degrees of grace, for God either is or is not gracious."[3] But the Scriptures declare that even within the confines of a single dis-

[2]Clarence B. Bass, *Backgrounds to Dispensationalism* (Grand Rapids: Wm. B. Eerdmans Publishing Co., 1960), p. 34.
[3]Daniel P. Fuller, "The Hermeneutics of Dispensationalism" (Doctor's dissertation, Northern Baptist Theological Seminary, Chicago, 1957), p. 164.

pensation God "giveth more [*meizon*] grace" (James 4:6).
Perhaps, then, there have been varying degrees of the display of God's grace throughout history, and perhaps it might even be proper to label one dispensation that of grace.

For another thing, nondispensationalists often misunderstand the entire concept of dispensations and often make them equivalent to ways of salvation. The stewardship may involve a revelation of the requirement for a right relation with God, but this is not all that is included in a dispensational arrangement. The use of the word *test* by dispensationalists in connection with stewardship responsibilities of a dispensation has undoubtedly given some cause for the charge.

But without question, the primary reason for the persistence of the charge has been the fact that dispensationalists have made unguarded statements which, if they were being made in the light of today's debate, would have been more carefully worded. Antidispensationalists are never quick to allow for refinement in the statement of dispensationalism, particularly if it dulls their attack. Scofield did write, "The point of testing is no longer legal obedience as the condition of salvation, but acceptance or rejection of Christ . . ."[4] But Scofield also wrote some other things, and what he would write today if he were alive and answering Bass or Fuller might be phrased differently.

Incidentally, nondispensationalists have made a few unguarded statements themselves about salvation under the Mosaic law. Allis wrote: "The Law is a declaration of the will of God for man's salvation."[5] Berkhof writes in one place: "Grace offers escape from the law only as a condition of salvation . . ." and in another place, "From the law . . . both as a means of obtaining eternal life and as a condemning

---

[4]The Scofield Reference Bible, p. 1115, note 2.
[5]Oswald T. Allis, *Prophecy and the Church* (Philadelphia: Presbyterian and Reformed Publishing Co., 1945), p. 39.

power believers are set free in Christ."[6] If, as these covenant theologians clearly state, the law was a means of salvation or of obtaining eternal life, then covenant theology must teach two ways of salvation—one by law and one through Christ. However, though these unguarded statements of covenant writers indicate two ways of salvation, we know full well that covenant theology insists on a single way of salvation, and it would not be fair to insist or imply otherwise. Similarly, antidispensationalists who seize on one unguarded statement of Scofield ought to have the same consideration and not leave the wrong impression. Dispensationalism does *not* teach two ways of salvation, and there are sufficient statements by dispensationalists to prove this fact. Let the opponents be fair and present the entire picture.

THE REPLY

The positive teaching of dispensational writers is that salvation is always through God's grace. Chafer asserted this position clearly when he wrote:

> Are there two ways by which one may be saved? In reply to this question it may be stated that salvation of whatever specific character is always the work of God in behalf of man and never a work of man in behalf of God. This is to assert that God never saved any one person or group of persons on any other ground than that righteous freedom to do so which the Cross of Christ secured. There is, therefore, but one way to be saved and that is by the power of God made possible through the sacrifice of Christ.[7]

In the latter years of his life Chafer was charged with teaching "various plans of salvation for various groups in various ages" by the General Assembly of the Presbyterian Church

[6]Louis Berkhof, *Systematic Theology* (Grand Rapids: Wm. B. Eerdmans Publishing Co., 1941), pp. 291, 614.
[7]L. S. Chafer, "Inventing Heretics Through Misunderstanding," *Bibliotheca Sacra*, 102 (January, 1945), 1.

in the U.S. In reply to the charge Chafer asserted in no uncertain terms:

> . . . The Editor has never held such views and . . . he
> yields first place to no man in contending that a holy
> God can deal with sin in any age on any other ground
> than that of the blood of Christ. The references cited by
> the Committee from the Editor's writings have no bear-
> ing on salvation whatever, but concern the rule of life
> which God has given to govern His people in the world.
> He has addressed a rule of life to Israel on the ground
> that they are His covenant people. Observing the rule
> of life did not make them covenant people. . . .[8]

It must be remembered that this statement was made in
direct answer to the charge that Chafer taught two ways of
salvation, and Chafer himself said that the other statements so
often quoted to show he taught two ways of salvation had no
bearing on that subject. May we not take him at his word as
being his own best interpreter, especially when he is speaking
to the specific point on which he was being attacked? In another place, and twenty years *before* the Presbyterian church
leveled the charge against him, Chafer said with equal clarity:
"The law was never given as a means of salvation or justification. . . ."[9]

Scofield, too, was equally clear that the Law was not a
means of salvation. He wrote: "Law neither justifies a sinner
nor sanctifies a believer."[10] And again he declared: "It is ex-
ceedingly important to observe . . . that the law is not
proposed as a means of life. . . ."[11]

Pettingill, another older dispensationalist, also declares
clearly: "Salvation has always been, as it is now, purely a gift

[8]L. S. Chafer, "Dispensational Distinctions Denounced," *Bibliotheca Sacra,*
101 (July, 1944), 259.
[9]L. S. Chafer, *Grace* (Findlay, Ohio: Dunham Publishing Co., 1922), p.
113.
[10]The Scofield Reference Bible, p. 1245.
[11]*Ibid.*, p. 93.

of God in response to faith. The dispensational tests served to show man's utter helplessness, in order to bring him to faith, that he might be saved by grace through faith plus nothing."[12]

These avowals of the single method of salvation by dispensationalists do not satisfy the nondispensationalists. The reason is simple: the nondispensationalist cannot reconcile such statements with the dispensationalists' distinction between law and grace. The problem partly goes back to the designations "law" and "grace" (which are entirely Biblical, Rom. 6:14). But it also stems from many antithetical statements which dispensationalists make concerning the distinctions between the economies which are, for better or for worse, designated "law" and "grace." One can see how important this matter of designation is by noting the different reaction and impression one receives by simply renaming the two economies the dispensation of Moses and the dispensation of Christ.

Nevertheless, covenant men still believe that dispensationalists are talking out of both sides of their mouths in this matter. Fuller calls these avowals of only one way of salvation in all the dispensations the new emphasis in dispensationalism, and he wants to know how it is to be harmonized with the duality of the way of salvation which he insists on seeing in Scofield and Chafer. He asks:

> How is this new emphasis in dispensationalism to be understood? Does it follow naturally from dispensationalism's hermeneutical basis? Or is it an idea that is simply superimposed on a structure that, otherwise, would teach in the manner of Scofield and Chafer? The answers to these questions are not easy to gain merely from listening to the contemporary dispensationalists, for as yet they have done little to show how this new

[12]William L. Pettingill, *Bible Questions Answered* (Wheaton, Ill.: Van Kampen Press, n.d.), p. 470.

emphasis rises naturally from their basic hermeneutical
approach. . . .[13]

His questioning is fair. Dispensationalism does need to
show in a systematic way how grace was displayed under the
Mosaic Law. We need not more brief statements that we
believe in only one way of salvation (though these should
not be ignored), but we need to expound the doctrine of
salvation under the law. As a friend and former student of
the writer said in his doctoral dissertation:

> Lamentable is the practice of dispensationalists who
> imagine that a simple categorical statement about salva-
> tion by grace through faith under the law suffices to
> meet the exigencies of the situation. . . . What dispen-
> sationalists must appreciate is that those who are not
> dispensationalists have difficulty understanding how
> they can hold salvation by faith and yet say what they
> say about the clean-cut distinction between grace and
> law. In other words, how is salvation by grace in the Old
> Testament to be reconciled with the Mosaic law viewed
> as an antithetical system of legal obedience and merit?
> This question must be answered not by expostulation
> but by exhibition, not by theoretical statements but by
> systematic theology. Moreover, any solution that omits
> the clear-cut distinction between law and grace will im-
> mediately be declared suspect by critical covenant con-
> troversialists.[14]

THE DOCTRINE OF GRACE

In stating the proper doctrine it is necessary to ask and
answer two questions: (1) What was the relation of the
Mosaic law to grace? (2) What grace was there under the
Mosaic law?

[13]Fuller, *op. cit.*, p. 157.
[14]H. Chester Woodring, "Grace Under the Mosaic Covenant" (Doctor's
dissertation, Dallas Theological Seminary, 1956), p. 208.

A. THE RELATION OF LAW AND GRACE

In relation to the first question, dispensationalists have given the impression that grace ended when the law was given at Sinai. A. C. Gaebelein wrote: "They had received grace, they needed grace. With the vow they made, they had put themselves under law."[15] Chafer, too, in his usual antithetical style, wrote in the same vein: "Israel deliberately forsook their position under grace, which had been their relation to God until that day, and placed themselves under the law."[16] Such statements and the inevitable impression given by charts of the dispensations present a picture of grace ending with the beginning of the Law. The implication has thus been made that because of this the Law was a retrogression in God's purpose.

If our concept of the dispensations be correct, then this is the wrong impression; for if the dispensations build on each other, then each one is an advance over the preceding one, culminating in the millennial state. How could this be so in the case of the Law? It is best seen by looking at the apostasy in Egypt with which the preceding dispensation ended. That apostasy proved that Israel needed a detailed code by which to live. Their need to be amalgamated into a nation also necessitated the giving of the law. Therefore, it was an advance in God's program for them, and not a retrogression into a legal system which the Israelites imposed upon themselves when in reality God wanted them to stay under grace.

The very giving of the law itself was that which made Israel famous among the nations (Deut. 4:6-8; 33:1-4). Furthermore, God did not give it because Israel deserved it, for her past actions had proved just the opposite. Her promotion to theocratic statehood was completely an act of grace, "and

[15]A. C. Gaebelein, *The Annotated Bible* (Wheaton: Van Kampen Press, 1913), I, 152.
[16]L. S. Chafer, *Systematic Theology* (Dallas: Seminary Press, 1947), IV, 162.

hence not a *suntheke*, a bargain between two equal parties, but a *diatheke*, a divinely ordained agreement."[17] From the very institution of the law Israel was not allowed to think or imagine that her privileged position was the result of her own meritorious action. The people were instructed to recognize it as a gift from God (Deut. 8:18). Reliance on the flesh was emphatically discouraged (Isa. 40:29-31; Zech. 4:6-7; Neh. 8:10). Thus the giving of the law did not abrogate grace. Paul's argument in Galatians 3:17-19 is simply that the law was never intended to annul any of the features of the Abrahamic covenant. It could not make void those promises; rather it was given to mark out the particular character of transgressions until the Seed, Jesus Christ, should come. The law was to lead the Israelites to Christ. In the accomplishing of these purposes for which the law was given, grace was not excluded, and for these purposes the law was "added alongside" the promise in order to advance Israel's relationship with God for that time.

In answer, then, to the first question as to the relation of the Mosaic law to grace, it was built upon what preceded without abrogating previously made promises, and it introduced a distinctive economy in God's dealings with the world. This is not double-talk, for we have already noted that a dispensation often incorporates features found in others. There is no reason, then, why the law should not incorporate grace and in no way change the promises made in a previous economy. After all, the promise to Noah concerning flooding the earth was not abrogated by succeeding dispensational arrangements. The law, too, was added alongside the promise made to Abraham (Gal. 3:14-18).

It is interesting to notice that the covenant theologian is not without problems in stating his view of the relationship between the law and his covenant of grace. He denies any

[17]E. Jauncey, *The Doctrine of Grace* (London, SPCK, 1925), p. 24. Cf. Gal. 4:24; II Cor. 6:14.

antithesis between the two, but at the same time he admits an antithesis. Berkhof describes the age of the Mosaic law in this manner:

> The Sinaitic covenant is an interlude, covering a period in which the real character of the covenant of grace, that is, its free and gracious character, is somewhat eclipsed by all kinds of external ceremonies and forms which, in connection with the theocratic life of Israel, placed the demands of the law prominently in the foreground (cf. Gal. 3). In the covenant with Abraham, on the other hand, the promise and the faith that responds to the promise are made emphatic.[18]

Thus all writers, of whatever theological persuasion, are sensitive to the antithetical nature of the law and grace and at the same time they all desire to maintain the doctrine of salvation by grace at all times. Both emphases are necessary, for there is an antithesis between the law and grace (or what do John 1:17, Rom. 6:14, and Gal. 3:23 mean?) and salvation has always been by grace.

B. THE DISPLAY OF GRACE UNDER THE LAW

The second question that needs to be considered is, What grace was there under the law? Do dispensationalists really teach that grace was present during the economy of the Mosaic Law?

In another book the writer has pointed out six ways in which grace was displayed under the Mosaic economy.[19] A brief summary of these will suffice to show that God did manifest grace during that dispensation and to answer the charge that dispensationalists do not teach grace was veiled under the Mosaic economy.

First, grace was displayed in electing Israel. This was an act of unmerited favor. This brought with it certain promises

[18]Berkhof, *op. cit.*, pp. 296-97.
[19]*The Grace of God* (Chicago: Moody Press, 1963), pp. 33-34.

which made available to the individual Israelite a multitude of blessings (Lev. 26:4-8; Deut. 7:14-16).

Second, grace was displayed in God's frequent restoration of His sinning people. The law had not even reached the people before it had been broken, and yet God, because of His grace, did not cast them off. During the conquest of Canaan, the lives of David and Solomon, and even during the captivities, God's grace was never absent from His people (Jer. 31:20; Hos. 2:19).

Third, the giving of the new covenant which was announced during the Law period was also a display of grace. The promise of a new age was given during the time when the law lay broken and trampled beneath the feet of the people who had proved themselves unworthy in every way (Jer. 31:32).

Fourth, God displayed His grace under the law by the enablement which He gave. Dispensationalists have often pictured the Law as a period when enablement was completely lacking.[20] It is true that there was a sharp contrast between the enablement under the law and the work of the Holy Spirit today (John 14:17), but it is not accurate to say there was no enablement under the law. The Spirit indwelt many (Dan. 4:8; I Pet. 1:11) and came upon many others for special power (Judges 3:10; I Sam. 10:9-10; Exodus 28:3), but there was no guarantee that He would permanently or universally indwell God's people as He does today.

Fifth, it was during the period of the Law that God revealed Himself in experience to His people as Yahweh. The name is associated with many specific acts of God's grace toward His people (Ps. 143:11; Jer. 14:21).

Sixth, the great covenant with David was made during the Mosaic economy, and its very institution was an act of great grace on God's part. The steadfast loving-kindness of God

[20]Chafer, *Systematic Theology*, IV, 247.

(*chesed*) is linked with the Abrahamic covenant (Micah 7:
20), with the Mosaic covenant (Exodus 34: 6-7), with the
new covenant (Jer. 31:3) and with the Davidic covenant
(Isa. 55:3). The covenant was not only established on God's
chesed, but David was assured that God's *chesed* would not
be thwarted and that the covenant would not be altered (Ps.
89:33-34). A promise like this was one of the most evident
displays of God's grace.

These displays of grace under the law did not lessen the
exacting demands of that law. The law did not cease to be
law simply because God was gracious during that economy.
Neither does this display of grace during that period lessen
the proper antithesis between the Mosaic economy and the
economy introduced by Christ. The Bible reveals the sharp
antithesis and at the same time asserts these displays of grace
during the Law dispensation. No system of theology can
ignore either emphasis, contradictory as they might seem,
even in the name of theological logic.

With his usual insight Sauer has caught these aspects of law
and grace and particularly grace under the law.

> Therefore even in the Old Testament the prophets and
> psalmists exult (Ps. 32:11; 33:1; 68:4) over the blessings
> and lifegiving effects of the Law. For them the Law was
> not only exposure of guilt and a leading on to despair
> (comp. Rom. 7), but "joy of heart" (Ps. 19:8), "de-
> light" (Ps. 119:47; 36:9), "bliss" (Ps. 32:1).
> "Knowledge of sin," says Paul (Rom. 3:20):
>   Of "crowning with grace" speaks David (Ps. 103:4).
> "The letter kills," says the apostle (II Cor. 3:6):
>   "The law is refreshing [quickening]," says the
>   psalmist (Ps. 19:8).
> "Miserable man!" is read in the epistle to the Romans
> (Rom. 7:24):
>   "Blessed is the man," says the Psalter (Ps. 1:1;
>   32:1).

Of the "curse," the one-time Pharisee speaks (Gal.
3:13) :

"The Lord bless thee," says the high priest (Num.
6:24) .[21]

THE DOCTRINE OF SALVATION

Pointing out these displays of grace, however, does not
solve the problem of salvation under the Mosaic law economy.
And it is a problem.

A. THE COVENANT POSITION

Covenant theology with its all-encompassing covenant of
grace does not have the solution. It has simplicity on its side,
for nothing could be more simple and nothing could seem-
ingly preserve the unity of the Bible better than simply to
say that all men are saved in exactly the same way during all
ages. And this is what covenant theology does say. Notice
Hodge's dogma: "The same Saviour, the same condition, the
same salvation."[22] A recent writer says in the same vein:
"There is but one, unified testament, God's sole plan of salvation, through which Christ offers a redemption that is equally
effective for the saints of both dispensations."[23]

These statements alone do not seem to be too inaccurate
until one realizes that covenant theologians always include in
their concept faith in Christ. Again Hodge asserts, "It was
not mere faith or trust in God, or simple piety, which was
required, but faith in the promised Redeemer, or faith in the
promise of redemption through the Messiah."[24] John 8:56,
Psalm 16:11, and Job 19:25-26 are always cited as proof texts,
and much is made of the illustrations of redemption in the
sacrificial system in the Old Testament. However, little is

[21]Erich Sauer, *The Dawn of World Redemption* (Grand Rapids: Wm.
B. Eerdmans Publishing Co., 1951), p. 133.
[22]Charles Hodge, *Systematic Theology* (London: Nelson, 1872), II, 368.
[23]J. Barton Payne, *The Theology of the Older Testament* (Grand Rapids:
Zondervan Publishing House, 1962), p. 241.
[24]Hodge, *op. cit.*, II, 366.

said of how much the Israelite understood what those illustrations represented. The reason for this is very plain—it is
very difficult if not impossible to prove that the *average*
Israelite understood the grace of God in Christ. Even Payne,
who labors in the book just cited to prove perception on the
part of Old Testament saints in order to reinforce the dogma
of the unity of salvation, admits in another book of his: "That,
to satisfy God, God must die, that men might inherit God, to
be with God, was *incomprehensible* under the Old Testament seminal knowledge of the Trinity, the incarnation, and
the crucifixion followed by the resurrection."[25] He can
apparently see more from a theological perspective than can
be seen from an historical viewpoint!

The obvious fallacy in the covenant theologian's solution
to this problem is that it is an a priori approach which has
yielded artificial results. The assumption is that everything
about salvation must be the same; therefore, the conscious
object of the faith of Old Testament saints must have been
Christ. This is not to imply that covenant theologians do
not recognize a limitation on the revelation of the Old
Testament, but they do everything possible to obliterate the
resulting effect that any limitation of revelation might have
on the doctrine of Old Testament salvation.

B. THE DISPENSATIONAL POSITION

The dispensationalists' answer to the problem is this: The
basis of salvation in every age is the death of Christ; the *requirement* for salvation in every age is faith; the *object* of faith
in every age is God; the *content* of faith changes in the various
dispensations. It is this last point, of course, which distinguishes dispensationalism from covenant theology, but it is
not a point to which the charge of teaching two ways of

[25]J. Barton Payne, *An Outline of Hebrew History* (Grand Rapids: Baker
Book House, 1954), p. 222 (italics in text mine).

salvation can be attached. It simply recognizes the obvious fact of progressive revelation. When Adam looked upon the coats of skins with which God had clothed him and his wife, he did not see what the believer today sees looking back on the cross of Calvary. And neither did other Old Testament saints see what we can see today. There have to be two sides to this matter—that which God sees from His side and that which man sees from his. This is what is meant by the Dallas Seminary doctrinal statement when it declares concerning this question of salvation:

> We believe that according to the "eternal purpose" of God (Eph. 3:11) salvation *in the divine reckoning* is always "by grace, through faith," and rests upon the shed blood of Christ. We believe that God has always been gracious, regardless of the ruling dispensation, but that man has not at all times been under an administration or stewardship of grace as is true in the present dispensation. . . . We believe . . . that the principle of faith was prevalent in the lives of all the Old Testament saints. However, we believe that it was historically impossible that they should have had as the conscious object of their faith the incarnate, crucified Son, the Lamb of God (John 1:29), and that it is evident that they did not comprehend as we do that the sacrifices depicted the person and work of Christ.[26]

For Fuller, this statement of the seminary is quite a problem.[27] But in reality it is a problem that does not exist except by his own creation. He simply has not distinguished the basis of salvation (which is by grace) from the content of revelation (which was not the same under the law as it is today). As has been pointed out, although God *is always gracious* He *does not always reveal grace* in the same manner

[26]Article V.
[27]Fuller, *op. cit.*, pp. 164-65.

or same amount. Different revelation does not affect His character. One must see two aspects to this entire matter—the unchanging basis of salvation in the grace of Christ and the changing content of revelation which affects the conscious object of faith. The covenant theologian does not see the latter and consequently raises his own problems, i. e., how to account for Biblical passages which do speak of the grace now operative as distinct from the grace which was operative during the Mosaic economy. John 1:17 does not mean that there was no grace before the coming of Christ, but it does mean that by comparison with the grace of Christ, all previous revelations of grace were as nothing. And this sharp antithesis the covenant theologian cannot harmonize with his unified doctrine of grace and unitized construction of the Bible. First Peter 1:10 does not mean there was no grace before the coming of Christ, but it does mean that there was grace which was never known or experienced by Old Testament saints in their lifetimes. Only dispensationalism can harmonize these two aspects of truth.

Another reason covenant theologians do not comprehend the dispensational answer is that they confuse the tests of a dispensation with the way of salvation. Capitalizing on the fact that most dispensationalists regard each dispensation as having a test, they equate the test with the way of salvation. Therefore it is easy for them to conclude that since each dispensation has its own test, and since there are several dispensations with their obvious differences, the dispensationalist must believe there are several different ways of salvation. There was a way of salvation revealed in each dispensation, and man's response to that particular revelation was *a* test of that economy. But there are many other tests in every dispensation. Every bit of revelation carries with it a test of whether man will respond positively or negatively to the particular thing revealed. One side of the coin is revelation or dispensation and the other side is responsibility or steward-ship.

Response to the revelation of the way of acceptance before God is but one test in any dispensation. Response to other aspects of the economy involves other tests. Under the law God provided a way whereby man could be eternally accept-able before Him. (The specifics of that way we have not yet discussed.) He also provided ways whereby man could be temporally acceptable before Him. Breaking the Sabbath was punishable by death. Keeping the Sabbath meant con-tinuance in the present life. But keeping the Sabbath did not mean eternal life. Therefore, it is entirely harmonious to say that the means of eternal salvation was by grace and the means of temporal life was by law. And it is also compatible to say that the revelation of the means of eternal salvation was through the law, and that that revelation (though it brought the same results when believed) was not the same as the revela-tion given since the incarnation of Christ. Thus the revelation concerning salvation during the Mosaic economy did involve the law though the basis of salvation remained grace.

This has to be the case, contradictory as it may seem. The law could not save, and yet the law was the revelation of God for that time. That the law could not save is perfectly clear. Men were saved under the law economy but not by the law. Scripture is plain concerning this fact—Romans 3:20 and II Corinthians 3:6-7. And yet the law contained the revelation which brought men to a realization that their faith must be placed in God the Saviour. How did it do this? Primarily through the worship which it instituted through the sacrifi-cial system. The sacrifices were part of the law; the keeping of them did not save; and yet a man could respond to what they taught so as to effect eternal salvation.

C. The Purpose of the Sacrifices

It is necessary, then, to examine more carefully this "gospel emphasis" in the sacrificial system. Is it clear enough to see the "same promise, the same Saviour, the same condition, the same salvation" as the covenant theologian believes? Or is it so limited as to change the content of faith as the dispensationalist says? To put the question theologically, it is simply this: What was the Christological content of the sacrificial system of the Mosaic law, and what relation did it have, if any, to Old Testament salvation?

Three views are generally held concerning the efficacy of the sacrifices which were instituted under the law. (1) Some hold that their efficacy extended to full remission of sins but such remission depended on the offerer having faith (since there was not inherent virtue in the sacrifices themselves). (2) Others believe that the efficacy of the Levitical sacrifices extended only to the remission of temporal penalties involved in the theocratic governmental setup of the nation Israel. This temporal remission was automatically effective whenever the offerer made a sacrifice, and did not depend on his having faith. He was "saved" from governmental penalties as long as he brought the offerings. (3) The third view combines ideas from the first two and holds that the sacrifices were automatically efficacious for theocratic forgiveness but were related to spiritual salvation only when offered in faith. Just how much knowledge was involved in that faith is undetermined.

Unquestionably the Old Testament does ascribe efficacy to the sacrifices. Again and again the Scriptures declare that when the sacrifices were offered according to the law "it shall be accepted for him to make an atonement for him" (Lev. 1:4; 4:26-31; 16:20-22). In none of these passages is there any indication that the effectiveness of the sacrifices depended on the spiritual state of the person offering them. Neither do the Scriptures imply that the offerer had to have some glimmer of understanding of the prefigurative purpose of these sacrifices for them to be effective for him. The face value interpretation of these passages assigns a genuine atonement for sins to the sacrifices simply because they were offered and not because the offerer was either worthy in himself or perceptive of something which the sacrifices pictured.

On the other hand, the New Testament is equally emphatic in asserting that "it is not possible that the blood of bulls and of goats should take away sin" (Heb. 10:4), and "the law having a shadow of good things to come, but not the very image of the things, can never with those sacrifices which they offered year by year continually make the comers thereunto perfect" (Heb 10:1). Such statements appear to be completely contradictory to those in the Old Testament.

The resolution of this apparent difficulty lies in distinguishing the primary relationship of sin in the Old Testament to that in the New. Under the law the individual Israelite by birth was related to God through the theocratic state. He sustained this relationship regardless of his spiritual state, and his relationship to the government had to include a certain relationship to the head of that government—God. There was no way in which he could disenfranchise himself, and as long as the government was theocratic there had to be a relation to God. When sin occurred, it was both a governmental and a spiritual offense because of the nature of a theocracy. Thus an Israelite's sin has to be viewed as "affecting the position and privileges of the offending party as a member of the . . . commonwealth of Israel."[28] All Israelites were related to God theocratically; some were also related spiritually. The bringing of the sacrifices restored the offender to his forfeited position as a Jewish worshiper and restored his theocratic relationship.

[28]T. J. Crawford, *The Doctrine of Holy Scripture Respecting the Atonement* (Grand Rapids: Baker Book House, 1954), p. 250.

In the present economy there is no theocracy, and thus there is no theocratic relationship between people and God. All relationships are direct and spiritual in contrast to governmental. Today a person's sin must be viewed in direct relationship to God, and the efficacy of the offering of Christ affects a person's spiritual relationship with God. The writer of the book of Hebrews does not say that sins were not forgiven by the Old Testament sacrifices, but he says that those sacrifices were inadequate to remove absolutely and finally the spiritual guilt of a person before God. This was done only by the death of Christ and not by the Levitical offerings. The offerings themselves could not automatically effect spiritual salvation.

But was this theocratic adjustment the only purpose of the offerings? Apparently not, for there seemed to have been in the offerings that which could point a believing worshiper to a better sacrifice which would deal finally with the entire sin question. This might be called an ulterior efficacy in the sacrifices which did not belong to them as sacrifices but as prefigurations of a final dealing with sin. However, it cannot be implied that the Israelite understood what that final dealing was. For if he had had sufficient insight to the extent of seeing and believing on the finished work of Christ, then he would not have had to offer the sacrifices annually, for he would have rested confidently in what he saw in the prefiguration. If the sacrifices had given a clear foreview of Christ, then the offerer would have understood the truth of a completed atonement and would not have had any conscience of sins every year. But since the Scriptures say that he did have conscience of sins, then he must not have seen very clearly "the same promise, the same Saviour, the same condition, and the same salvation" as the believer today sees. And if so, then the covenant position is an historical anachronism, a reading back of the New Testament revelation into the Old, and a failure to recognize the progress of revelation and the distinctions of the differences of God's economies. Christ was not the conscious object of their faith, though they were saved by faith in God as He had revealed Himself principally through the sacrifices which He instituted as a part of the Mosaic law.

This conclusion is exactly the teaching of the New Testament. On Mars Hill Paul summarized the Old Testament understanding of salvation and called the period "the times of this ignorance" at which God "winked" (Acts 17:30). This does not reflect very clear comprehension of the Christological content of their faith! Paul again summarized the situation concerning salvation in the Old Testament as "remission of sins that are past through the forbearance of God" (Rom. 3:25). The understanding of the average Israelite concerning Messiah at the time Jesus walked the earth was very feeble (John 1:21; 7:40), and even the prophets lacked comprehension (I Pet. 1:10-11). These passages make it impossible to say that Old Testament saints under the law exercised personal faith in Jesus Christ.

SUMMARY AND CONCLUSION

The charge of the covenant theologian that dispensationalism teaches two ways of salvation is based on what he thinks ought to be the logical teaching of dispensationalism, rather than what is the actual teaching of dispensationalism. It is a charge which arises partly from the antithetical nature of the Mosaic period and the period of grace and truth through Jesus Christ. However much the covenant theologian might wish to put every dealing of God into the straitjacket of his covenant of grace, he himself admits that there is an antithetical dealing of God in the administration of the law. While dispensationalists may have overemphasized the differences between law and grace, the covenant man has failed to admit differences.

In order to show that dispensationalism does not teach several ways of salvation, we emphasized (1) the fact that the law was brought in alongside and did not abrogate the promises of the Abrahamic covenant, and (2) the fact that there were many displays of grace under the law. Dispensationalism alone among theological systems teaches both the antithetical nature of law and grace and the truth of grace under the law (and incidentally, law under grace). Grace was shown to be displayed in several ways, but the crux of the matter was the display of grace in salvation.

In examining salvation under the Mosaic law the principal question is simply, How much of what God was going to do in the future did the Old Testament believer comprehend? According to both Old and New Testament revelation it is impossible to say that he saw the same promise, the same Saviour as we do today. Therefore, the dispensationalists' distinction between the *content* of his faith and the content of ours is valid. The basis of salvation is always the death of Christ; the means is always faith; the object is always God (though man's understanding of God before and after the incarnation is obviously different) ; but the content of faith depends on the particular revelation God was pleased to give at a certain time. These are the distinctions which the dispensationalist recognizes, and they are distinctions necessitated by plain interpretation of revelation as it was given.

If by two "ways" of salvation is meant different content of faith, then dispensationalism does teach two ways because the Scriptures teach thus. But if by "ways" is meant two bases or means, then dispensationalism most emphatically does not teach two ways. One simply must recognize the component parts of salvation regardless of what this recognition may do to the covenant of grace.

7

THE CHURCH IN
DISPENSATIONALISM

THE NATURE OF THE CHURCH is a crucial point of difference between dispensationalism and other doctrinal viewpoints. Indeed, ecclesiology, or the doctrine of the Church, is the touchstone of dispensationalism. Not only has the dispensational teaching concerning the Church been the subject of controversy, but also the ramifications of that teaching in ecclesiastical life have been attacked. Antidispensationalists, rather than examining the validity of the dispensational teaching on this subject, simply dismiss it as heretical because they know of this or that instance where some dispensationalist was connected with a local church split. Bass is quite accurate, however, in stating that "whatever evaluation history may make of this movement, it will attest that dispensationalism is rooted in Darby's concept of the church—a concept that sharply distinguishes the church from Israel . . ."[1] But he is quite unscholarly in making his chief criticism of Darby's doctrine the "practical effects, rather than . . . theological arguments."[2] We must be constantly reminded that the test of any doctrine is whether or not it is Scriptural. It is probably safe to say that most doctrines have been abused in practice, so that if tested by their

[1]Clarence B. Bass, *Backgrounds to Dispensationalism* (Grand Rapids: Wm. B. Eerdmans Publishing Co., 1960), p. 127.
[2]*Ibid.*

practical effects they would all have to be discarded. Nevertheless, this doctrine of the Church is a decisive one in dispensationalism and must be examined as to its Scriptural accuracy.

THE DISTINCTIVENESS OF THE CHURCH

A. THE CHURCH HAS A DISTINCT CHARACTER

The distinct character of the Church is found in its unique relationship to the living Christ as the Body of which He is the Head. ". . . and gave him to be the head over all things to the church, which is his body, the fullness of him that filleth all in all" (Eph. 1:22-23). "And he is the head of the body, the church" (Col. 1:18). "Now ye are the body of Christ, and members in particular" (I Cor. 12:27).

The distinctiveness of the character of the Church as the Body of Christ is twofold. It is distinct because of who are included within that body (i.e., Jews and Gentiles), and it is distinct because of the new relationship of Christ indwelling the members of that body. Both of these distinctives are unique with the Church and were not known or experienced by God's people in Old Testament times.

The inclusion of Jews and Gentiles in the same body is a mystery, the content of which is "that the Gentiles are fellow-heirs, and fellow-members of the body, and fellow-partakers of the promise in Christ Jesus through the gospel" (Eph. 3:6, ASV). This is a mystery "which in other ages was not made known unto the sons of men, as it is now revealed unto his holy apostles and prophets by the Spirit" (Eph. 3:5).

The amillennialist tries to undermine the importance of this declaration by insisting that the word *as* in verse 5 shows that this mystery was partially revealed in Old Testament times and therefore is not distinctive to the Church age.[3]

[3]Oswald T. Allis, *Prophecy and the Church* (Philadelphia: Presbyterian and Reformed Publishing Co., 1945), pp. 90-110.

Even if the *as* could be so construed, this does not mean that the body composed of Jews and Gentiles was in existence in Old Testament times. Paul has just written in the same Ephesian epistle that only in Christ was the middle wall of partition broken down between Jew and Gentile so that He could "reconcile both unto God in one body by the cross" (Eph. 2:16). This was not done before the cross; therefore, it is clear that the new man, the one body, was not in existence in Old Testament times. Even if it had been partially revealed, as Allis claims, that did not bring it into existence. The Body of Christ could not have been constituted until after the death of Christ, and the time of the revelation of that truth does not affect the institution of it. The Old Testament does predict Gentile blessing for the millennial period (Isa. 61:5-6; 2:1-4), but the specific blessings do not include equality with the Jews as is true today in the Body of Christ. Great blessing is promised Gentiles in the predictions of the Old Testament, but not on the basis of equality of position with the Jews. This equality is the point of the mystery revealed to the apostles and prophets in New Testament times.[4]

[4]The implication that the "as" clause in Ephesians 3:5 might imply a partial revelation in the Old Testament has been allowed to stand only for the sake of argument. That it does not imply this has been made perfectly clear in John F. Walvoord's discussion of this passage in *The Millennial Kingdom* (Findlay, Ohio: Dunham Publishing Co., 1959), pp. 232-37. He points out that the "as" clause is not restrictive (qualifying the preceding statement, as Allis hopes) but it is adjectival (merely giving additional information), the "as" itself being purely descriptive and not qualifying. He also calls attention to the rather amazing omission by Allis of any discussion of the similar passage in Col. 1:26 where the mystery is stated in no uncertain terms as completely hidden. A quotation from James M. Stifler, *The Epistle to the Romans, a Commentary Logical and Historical* (Chicago: Moody Press, 1960), p. 254, is worth reproducing here, for it states the matter explicitly: ". . . The contrast here, as Colossians 1:26 shows, is between the other ages and 'now.' It may be further remarked on this Ephesian passage that the 'as' does not give a comparison between degrees of revelation in the former time and 'now.' It denies that there was any revelation at all of the mystery in that former time; just as if one should tell a man born blind that the sun does not shine in the night as it does in the daytime. It does not shine at all by night. Certainly there is no comparison by 'as' in Acts 2:15; . . . 'As' with a negative in the preceding clause has not received the attention which it deserves. It is sometimes almost equivalent to 'but' (I Cor. 7:31)."

The other aspect of the distinctiveness of the character of the Church as the Body of Christ is the indwelling presence of Christ in the members of that body. This is the mystery revealed in Colossians 1:27: "To whom God would make known what is the riches of the glory of this mystery among the Gentiles; which is Christ in you, the hope of glory." This mystery is expressly said to have "been hid from ages and from generations, but now is made manifest to his saints" (Col. 1:26). The immediate context speaks of the Body of Christ three times (vv. 18, 22, 24), leaving no doubt that it is the members of the body who are indwelt by the living Christ. This is what makes the body a living organism, and this relationship was unknown in Old Testament times.

The Church as a living organism in which Jew and Gentile are on an equal footing is the mystery revealed only in New Testament times and able to be made operative only after the cross of Christ. This is the distinct character of the Church—a character which was not true of the body of Old Testament saints.

B. The Church Has a Distinct Time

It is quite evident from what has just been said that the dispensational understanding of the Church limits its building to this present age. It was something unknown in Old Testament times; it is a distinct entity in this present age.

The proofs of the distinctiveness of the Church to this age are three.

First, there is the proof from the mystery character of the Church. This is the natural corollary of what has been discussed in the preceding section. If the distinctive character of the Church as a living organism indwelt by Christ in which Jews and Gentiles are on an equal basis is described as a mystery unknown in Old Testament times, then the Church must not have been constituted in those Old Testament days.

Indeed, Paul says very clearly that this entity is a "new man" (Eph. 2:15) made possible only after the death of Christ.

Second, the Church is distinctive to this age because of what Paul has to say about the beginning and completion of the Church. Concerning its beginning, Paul is emphatic in placing stress on the necessary relation of the Church to the resurrection and ascension of Christ. It is built upon His resurrection, for the Lord was made Head of the Church after God "raised him from the dead, and set him at his own right hand in the heavenlies" (Eph. 1:20; cf. vv. 22-23). Furthermore, the proper functioning and operation of the Church is dependent upon the giving of gifts to the body, and the giving of gifts is, in turn, dependent upon the ascension of Christ (Eph. 4:7-12). If by some stretch of the imagination the Body of Christ could be said to have been in existence before the ascension of Christ, then it would have to be concluded that it was a nonoperating body. In Paul's thought the Church is built on the resurrection and ascension, and that means it is distinctive to this age. Concerning the completion of the Church when saints will be translated and resurrected, Paul uses the phrase "dead in Christ" (I Thess. 4:16). This clearly distinguishes those who have died in this age from believers who died before Christ's first advent, thus marking the Church off as distinct to this age and a mystery hidden in Old Testament times but not revealed.

Third, the baptizing work of the Holy Spirit proves that the Church did not begin until Pentecost. The Lord had spoken of this work of the Spirit just before His ascension (Acts 1:5) as being yet future and unlike anything they had previously experienced. Although it is not expressly recorded in Acts 2 that the baptism of the Spirit occurred on the day of Pentecost, it is said in Acts 11:15-16 that it did happen on that day in fulfillment of the promise of the Lord as recorded in 1:5. Paul later explained the doctrinal significance of the baptism as placing people into the Body of Christ (I Cor. 12:13). In other words, on the day of Pentecost men were first placed into the Body of Christ. Since the Church is the Body of Christ (Col. 1:18), the Church could not have begun until Pentecost, and it had to begin on that day.

The distinctiveness of the Church to this age as emphasized in dispensationalism does not mean (1) that dispensationalists believe there were no people rightly related to God in Old Testament times, or (2) that Christ is not the Founder of the Church. All that was said in Chapter 6 concerning salvation in the Old Testament shows clearly the dispensational position concerning Old Testament saints. Nevertheless, dispensationalism insists that the people of God who have been baptized into the Body of Christ and who thus form the Church are distinct from saints of other days or even of a future time. Dispensationalists fully recognize that the Church is Christ's Church (Matt. 16:18). He chose and trained its first leaders during His earthly ministry. Some of His teaching was in anticipation of the formation of the Church. His death, resurrection, ascension and exaltation were the necessary foundation on which the Church was to be built. But although the Lord is the Founder of the Church and the one who laid the groundwork during His earthly life, the Church did not come into functional and operational existence until the day of Pentecost. It is distinctive to this time.

C. THE CHURCH IS DISTINCT FROM ISRAEL

All nondispensationalists blur to some extent the distinction between Israel and the Church. Such blurring fails to recognize the contrast that is maintained in Scripture between Israel, the Gentiles, and the Church. In the New Testament natural Israel and the Gentiles are contrasted. Israel is addressed as a nation in contrast to Gentiles *after* the Church was established at Pentecost (Acts 3:12; 4:8, 10; 5:21, 31, 35; 21:28). In Paul's prayer for natural Israel (Rom. 10:1) there is a clear reference to Israel as a national people as distinct from and outside the Church.

Further, natural Israel and the Church are also contrasted in the New Testament. Paul wrote: "Give none offense, neither to the Jews, nor to the Gentiles, nor to the church of God" (I Cor. 10:32). If the Jewish people were the same group as the Church or the Gentiles, then certainly there would be no point in the apostle's distinction in this passage. Too, Paul, obviously referring to natural Israel as his "kinsmen according to the flesh," ascribes to them the covenants and the promises (Rom. 9:3-4). The fact that these words were written after the beginning of the Church is proof that the Church does not rob Israel of her blessings. The term *Israel* continues to be used for the natural (not spiritual) descendants of Abraham after the Church was instituted, and it is not equated with the Church.

In addition, believing Jews and believing Gentiles, which together make up the Church in this age, continue to be distinguished in the New Testament, proving that the term *Israel* still means the physical descendants of Abraham. Romans 9:6, "For they are not all Israel, which are of Israel," does not say that the spiritual remnant within Israel is the Church. It simply distinguishes the nation as a whole from the believing element *within the nation*. This kind of distinction within the nation was often made in the Old Testament and thus would be familiar to Jews reading such a statement as Romans 9:6. The servant of the Lord in the Old Testament is sometimes called "blind" and "deaf" (Isa. 42:19) and sometimes the term obviously refers to the righteous remnant within Israel (Isa. 44:1; 51:1, 7). In the Romans passage Paul is reminding his readers that being an Israelite by natural birth does not assure one of the life and favor promised the believing Israelite who approached God by faith.

More frequently nondispensationalists use Galatians 6:15-16 to attempt to show that the Church is the new, spiritual Israel. Paul wrote: "For in Christ Jesus neither circumcision availeth any thing, nor uncircumcision, but a new creature. And as many as walk according to this rule, peace be on them, and mercy, and upon the Israel of God." The question is, Who is the Israel of God? The amillennialist insists that these verses teach that the Israel of God is the entire Church. The premillennialist says that Paul is simply singling out Christian Jews for special recognition in the benediction but not equating them with the whole Church.

Grammar in this instance does not decide the matter for us. The "and" in the phrase "and upon the Israel of God" can be explicative; that is, it can mean "even," in which case the phrase "Israel of God" would be a synonym for the "new creature" and would thus make the Church the Israel of God. Lenski is typical of those who so interpret the passage. He says: " 'As many as will keep in line with the rule,' constitute 'the Israel of God.' "[5] On the other hand, if the "and" is understood in an emphatic sense, then it has the meaning of "adding a (specially important) part to the whole" and is translated "and especially" (cf. Mark 16:7; Acts 1:14).[6] The "and" might also be a simple connective which would also distinguish the Israel of God as Jewish Christians but not identify them as the whole Church. The connective force would be less emphatic than the "especially" meaning, but both interpretations would distinguish Jewish and Gentile believers. Only the explicative interpretation ("even") identifies the Church and Israel.

[5]R. C. H. Lenski, *The Interpretation of St. Paul's Epistles to the Galatians, to the Ephesians, and to the Philippians* (Columbus: Wartburg Press, 1946), p. 321.

[6]William F. Arndt and F. Wilbur Gingrich, *A Greek-English Lexicon of the New Testament* (Chicago: University of Chicago Press, 1957), p. 392.

While the grammar cannot of itself decide the question, the argument of the book of Galatians does favor the connective or emphatic meaning of "and." Paul had strongly attacked the Jewish legalists; therefore, it would be natural for him to remember with a special blessing those Jews who had forsaken this legalism and followed Christ and the rule of the new creation. One might also ask why, if the New Testament writers meant to equate clearly Israel and the Church, they did not do so plainly in the many other places in their writings where they had convenient opportunity to do so.

Use of the words *Israel* and *Church* shows clearly that in the New Testament national Israel continues with her own promises and the Church is never equated with a so-called "new Israel" but is carefully and continually distinguished as a separate work of God in this age.

D. THE COVENANT THEOLOGY TEACHING ON THE DISTINCTIVENESS OF THE CHURCH

The covenant theologian denies the distinctiveness of the Church to this present age. His viewpoint is based on his premise that God's program for the world is the salvation of individuals; therefore, the saved people of God in all ages may be called the Church. If the Church is God's redeemed people of all ages, then the Church must have begun with Adam, though most covenant writers are reluctant to say that. They usually begin the Church with Abraham in order to found it on the Abrahamic covenant, link it to the olive tree of Romans 11, preserve the idea of a group fellowship, and be able to use the label "Israel" for the Church. The Church in the New Testament is the "new Israel," and the Church in the Old Testament is Israel. But before Abraham what was the Church? Berkhof, however, does recognize the Church as existing in godly families before the calling out of

Abraham.[7] Would one call this phase of the Church the "pre-Israel" Church?

The covenant amillennialist defines the Church as "a congregation or an assembly of the people of God. . . ."[8] In this view there is no real difference between the Church in the Old and in the New Testaments. ". . . the Church existed in the old dispensation as well as in the new, and was *essentially* the same in both, in spite of acknowledged institutional and administrative differences."[9] To the covenant amillennialist the Church is the people of God in every age, whether pre-Israel, Israel, or new Israel.

Covenant premillennialists see no distinction in God's purpose until the millennium suddenly begins, and they do not agree as to who are included in the Church. Payne apparently accepts completely the covenant concept of the Church in the Old Testament, particularly beginning with Abraham and culminating in the "new Israel" in the New Testament.[10] Ladd takes a viewpoint very near that of the dispensationalist.

> There is therefore but one people of God. This is not to say that the Old Testament saints belonged to the Church and that we must speak of the Church in the Old Testament. Acts 7:38 does indeed speak of the "church in the wilderness"; but the word here does not bear its New Testament connotation but designates only the "congregation" in the wilderness. The Church properly speaking had its birthday on the day of Pentecost, for the Church is composed of all those who by one Spirit have been baptized into one body (I Cor. 12:13),

[7]Louis Berkhof, *Systematic Theology* (Grand Rapids: Wm. B. Eerdmans Publishing Co., 1941), p. 570.
[8]*Ibid.*, p. 571.
[9]*Ibid.*
[10]J. Barton Payne, *The Theology of the Older Testament* (Grand Rapids: Zondervan Publishing House, 1962), p. 91. It is interesting to notice that Payne recognizes that natural Israel is distinguished from the Church, p. 483.

and this baptizing work of the Spirit began on the day of Pentecost.[11]

Fuller insists on one people of God while recognizing some distinction in the terms "Israel" and "the Church." He says:

> Thus it appears that the olive tree analogy yields the natural interpretation that there is but one people of God throughout redemptive history. Prior to the Cross, this people was composed largely of Jews who through faith and obedience inherited the promises made to Abraham. Since the Cross, this group has comprised Gentiles who are made equally the heirs of the promises to Abraham. The term "Church" applies properly only to that group since the Cross, just as "Israel" applies properly to the group before the Cross and to the ethnic entity who traces its descent from Abraham.[12]

In other words, Fuller sees the one redeemed people as beginning with Abraham. What about those who were rightly related to God and who lived before Abraham? They would not have been heirs of the "promises made to Abraham" later, and yet they were redeemed. Do they (like the family of Noah) represent another people of God with different promises from those given to Abraham? He also sees the New Testament Church as part of that continuing redeemed people and yet somewhat distinct. Here again is seen the inconsistency in application of the literal principle of interpretation in the covenant premillennialist's position.

In relation to pre-Abrahamic saints, another question may be asked. If God was saving people before the call of Abraham, then why did He call out and mark off a national group? If spiritual salvation was being experienced by people before

[11]G. E. Ladd, *The Gospel of the Kingdom* (Grand Rapids: Wm. B. Eerdmans Publishing Co., 1959), p. 117.
[12]Daniel P. Fuller, "The Hermeneutics of Dispensationalism" (Doctor's dissertation, Northern Baptist Theological Seminary, Chicago, 1957), p. 362.

Abraham, why not carry on this redemptive work in the same manner without the national distinction which was made when Israel was singled out from the other nations? The very calling out of Israel must indicate some national purpose for that nation as well as the continuing of the work of spiritual salvation. Certainly one cannot say that the New Testament Church is national Israel fulfilling the promises given to that nation. Therefore, one must conclude that the Church is not the continuation of Israel and her purpose in being called out from among the nations. Even the covenant premillennialist admits that the national promises to Israel are not fulfilled by the Church (he reserves their fulfillment for the millennial period), but he will not conclude that God might have a different purpose entirely in the calling out of the Church. He is completely blinded by the premise that the one death of Christ must mean one people of God saved in the same way and called out for the same purpose.

Let it be said very emphatically at this point that dispensationalism does not deny that God has His own redeemed people throughout all ages. But that these constitute *a* people rather than peoples of God we do deny. The fact that God saved people from among the Israelites and the fact that God saves people from among Gentiles today does not make the Church equal to Israel or make the Church the fulfillment of Israel's purposes and promises. This does not follow any more than the fact that God saved Noah and his family and the fact that God saved Israelites make Israel the family of Noah or make Israel to fulfill the purposes of Noah. Israel is distinct from the godly line that preceded the calling out of Abraham and Israel's promises were different. The godly from both groups are redeemed, but they do not necessarily have the same promises or fulfill the same purposes. The same is true in comparing Israel and the Church. But such obvious and necessary distinctions the covenant theologian (whether premillennial or amillennial) fails to recognize. He has formed a mold into which he pours all the redeemed, and nothing, not even Scripture, must break it. That God is continuing His work of redemption in calling out a people for His name in the Church the Body of Christ we gladly affirm, but we also insist that this Body of Christ is distinct from any previous body of redeemed people in its nature, characteristics, time, and promises.

THE RELATIONSHIPS OF THE CHURCH

The truth of the distinctiveness of the Church does not deny the fact that she has relationships with other purposes of God. Although dispensationalists recognize the Church as distinct in the plan of God, this does not mean that she is isolated from the plan of God. The Church is related and integrated in the plan of God while maintaining her distinctive purpose. These ideas are not contradictory, and both sides of the coin need to be examined.

A. The Relation of the Church to the Kingdom

Because of the sharp distinction dispensationalists draw between the purpose of God in the Church and His purpose in the kingdom, it is often assumed that there is no relationship between the two. In relation to the future millennial kingdom, dispensationalists have always taught that the Church will share in the rule of that kingdom. Chafer believed that the Church would "reign with Him on the earth."[13] Sauer pictured the Church as the "ruling aristocracy, the official administrative staff, of the coming kingdom."[14] At the same time dispensationalists maintain the separate place and distinct blessings of national Israel restored and regener-

---

[13]L. S. Chafer, *Dispensationalism* (Dallas: Seminary Press, 1936), p. 30.
[14]Erich Sauer, *From Eternity to Eternity* (London: Paternoster Press, 1954), p. 93.

ated in the millennial kingdom. The Church, while distinct in the millennial kingdom, is not apart from it.

In relation to this present age and the kingdom in mystery, the position of believers in the Church is well summarized by Sauer:

> As to their persons they are citizens of the kingdom; as to their existence they are the fruit of the message of the kingdom; as to their nature they are the organism of the kingdom; as to their task they are the ambassadors of the kingdom.[15]

In the same vein Pentecost writes:

> During this present age, then, while the King is absent, the theocratic kingdom is in abeyance in the sense of its actual establishment on the earth. Yet it remains as the determinative purpose of God. Paul declared this purpose when he was "preaching the kingdom of God" (Acts 20:25). Believers have been brought into "the kingdom of his dear Son" (Col. 1:13) through the new birth. Unbelievers are warned they will not have part in that kingdom (I Cor. 6:9-10; Gal. 5:21; Eph. 5:5). Others were seen to have labored with Paul "unto the kingdom of God" (Col. 4:11). . . . Such references, undoubtedly, are related to the eternal kingdom and emphasize the believer's part in it.[16]

How can the Church be distinct from the kingdom purpose and yet be related to it? We must not try to understand such a seeming paradox by obliterating the distinction between the two purposes (as the antidispensationalist does) any more than such a procedure would satisfactorily harmonize sovereignty and responsibility. The truth must stand even though it may seem to involve paradox to the human mind. And yet if our concept of the kingdom were as broad as it appears

[15]*Ibid.*, pp. 92-93.
[16]J. Dwight Pentecost, *Things to Come* (Findlay, Ohio: Dunham Publishing Co., 1958), p. 471.

to be in the Scriptures and our definition of the Church as strict as it is in the Scriptures, perhaps nondispensationalists would cease trying to equate the Church with the kingdom and dispensationalists would speak more of the relationship between the two.

B. The Relation of the Church to Saints of Other Ages

Again because of the distinction between God's purpose in the Church and His purpose for Israel, dispensationalists are thought to teach that the Israelitish saints have no heavenly hope or future. Dispensationalists have sometimes made a sharp distinction between the heavenly future of the Church and the earthly future for national Israel. For instance, Chafer wrote:

> The dispensationalist believes that throughout the ages God is pursuing two distinct purposes; one related to the earth with earthly people and earthly objectives involved, which is Judaism; while the other is related to heaven with heavenly people and heavenly objectives involved, which is Christianity.[17]

Any apparent dichotomy between heavenly and earthly purposes is not actual. The earthly purpose of Israel of which dispensationalists speak concerns the national promise which will be fulfilled by Jews during the millennium as they live on the earth in *un*resurrected bodies. The earthly future for Israel does not concern Israelites who die before the millennium is set up. The destiny of those who die is different. Believing Israelites of the Mosaic age who died in faith have a heavenly destiny. Unbelieving ones will be confined in the lake of fire. Jews today who believe in Christ are members of the Church, His Body, and their destiny is the same as Gentile believers. But to those Jews who will be living on the earth in earthly bodies when the millennium

[17]*Op. cit.*, p. 107.

begins and to those who will be born with earthly bodies during the period will be fulfilled the earthly promises which
have remained unfulfilled during these years. Even during
the days of the millennial kingdom there will be those who
believe and those who reject the Saviour-King, and their
eternal destiny will be determined by their heart relationship
to Him. But until they die or until the millennium ends,
their destiny will be to fulfill those earthly promises of the
Abrahamic and Davidic covenants.

But that dispensationalism denies a heavenly hope and
future for Israel is simply not true. Many dispensational
writers as well as others recognize this heavenly place for Old
Testament saints in the assertion of Hebrews 12:22-23:

> But ye are come unto mount Sion, and unto the city of
> the living God, the heavenly Jerusalem, and to an in-
> numerable company of angels, to the general assembly
> and church of the firstborn, which are written in heaven,
> and to God the Judge of all, and to the spirits of just
> men made perfect.

They understand "the spirits of just men made perfect" to
refer to Old Testament believers who have their place in
the heavenly city along with the Church of firstborn ones.[18]
Their eternal place in the heavenly Jerusalem is certain, and
in that heavenly state they are distinguished from the Church!
Distinction is maintained even though the destiny is the same.

To sum up: the earthly-heavenly, Israel-Church distinction
taught by dispensationalists is true, but it is not everything
that dispensationalists teach about the ultimate destiny of
the people included in these groups. Pentecost has summarized the whole picture well.

> The conclusion to this question would be that the Old
> Testament held forth a national hope, which will be

[18]Cf. William Kelly, *Exposition of the Epistle to the Hebrews* (London:
Weston, 1905), pp. 250-51.

realized fully in the millennial age. The individual Old Testament saint's hope of an eternal city will be realized through resurrection in the heavenly Jerusalem, where, without losing distinction or identity, Israel will join with the resurrected and translated of the church age to share in the glory of His reign forever. The nature of the millennium, as the period of the test of fallen humanity under the righteous reign of the King, precludes the participation by resurrected individuals in that testing. Thus the millennial age will be concerned only with men who . . . are living in their natural bodies.[19]

C. THE RELATION OF THE CHURCH TO THE SEED OF ABRAHAM

Nondispensationalists, particularly amillennialists, often argue that since the Church is the seed of Abraham and Israel is the seed of Abraham, the Church equals Israel. What is the relation of the Church to the concept of the seed of Abraham? In a word, the answer is this: the Church is *a* seed of Abraham, but this does not mean that the Church is Israel.

The entire matter is clarified by the simple realization that the Scriptures speak of more than one kind of seed born to Abraham. (1) There is the natural seed, the physical descendants of Abraham—"But thou, Israel, art my servant, Jacob whom I have chosen, the seed of Abraham my friend" (Isa. 41:8). (2) There is Christ—"Now to Abraham and his seed were the promises made. He saith not, And to seeds, as of many; but as of one, And to thy seed, which is Christ" (Gal. 3:16). (3) Christians are Abraham's seed—"And if ye be Christ's, then are ye Abraham's seed, and heirs according to the promise" (Gal. 3:29).

In general the amillennialist minimizes the physical seed aspect. Premillennialists, whether dispensationalists or covenant, recognize the physical seed as well as the spiritual seed, but the covenant premillennialist agrees with the amillennialist in equating Israel and the Church. The crux of the matter is this: Is the spiritual seed of Abraham also called Israel?

It is quite obvious that Christians are called the spiritual seed of Abraham, but the New Testament nowhere says that they are the heirs of the national promises made to the physical descendants. It is this recognition of the future fulfillment of these promises to natural Israel that makes a man a premillennialist in contrast to an amillennialist. But the term *Israel* is not the appellative given to the spiritual seed of Abraham. It is correct to call *some* of the spiritual seed of Abraham spiritual Israel, but not all. Faithful, believing Jews in Old Testament times were spiritual Israel and both the physical and spiritual seed of Abraham. But faith, not race, is the determinative reason for being able to be called the spiritual seed of Abraham. Only when a believer belongs to the race Israel can he in any sense be called a spiritual Israelite.

To carry this designation *Israel* over to believers in the Church is not warranted by the New Testament. It is interesting to note that those who want to do this and thus to try to make Israel equal to the Church do not carry the same principle back before the time of the delineation of Israel as a nation. Abraham was justified when he was neither a Gentile nor a Jew and when he represented the whole of mankind, not merely the Jewish people. Before Israel ever came into being as a nation, Abraham became the pattern for the justification of all men including those who would believe from among the Jewish nation that would arise later. Faith and justification are personal and individual matters, and belonging to the spiritual seed of Abraham is also a personal and individual matter unrelated to race. The spiritual seed of Abraham does not mean Israel, for Abraham is related to Israel as a national father, and he is related to believing individuals of all nations (including the Jewish) who believe, as a spiritual father. But believers *as a group* are not called spiritual Israel.

D. The Relation of the Church to Apostasy

Most opponents of dispensationalism attack in one way or another the dispensational teaching concerning apostasy in the church. Chamberlain, representing the faculty of the Louisville Presbyterian Theological Seminary, wrote concerning the doctrine of the apostate church: "Dispensationalism appears in its most vicious form in this doctrine."[20] Then he goes on to cite two cases from his own experience in which churches were split because of dispensational teaching. Only after citing these examples, which would inevitably involve his readers emotionally in the matter, does he examine any Biblical data. He dismisses the teaching of the central passages, I Timothy 4 and II Timothy 3, by asserting that they were "intended to guide Christians in Ephesus in the first century."[21]

Similarly, Bass begins and ends his chapter on Darby's doctrine of the Church with criticisms of the emphasis on apostasy. There is little, if any other, criticism of Darby's doctrine in this area except as it affects separatism.[22]

Most people, like Chamberlain, cannot discuss the doctrine without being emotionally involved in some practical case. Many also reason that if the effect (the practical instance they experienced) was so bad, then certainly the cause (dispensational teaching) must be heretical. This makes it difficult to discuss the subject objectively, but this is what must be done. After all, if every doctrine that brought division among professing Christians were condemned on that score, then

[20]W. D. Chamberlain, *The Church Faces the Isms* (New York: Abingdon Press, 1958), p. 106.
[21]*Ibid.*, p. 108.
[22]*Op. cit.*, pp. 100-127.

most doctrines would have to be judged heretical. Many Christians today are divided over the matter of the inspiration of the Bible. Does this make inspiration a dangerous doctrine which should be rejected because it has caused divisions? Such things ought to drive us to the Scriptures to see what is really taught, and the same is true of the doctrine of apostasy.

Basically there are two questions concerning apostasy which must be answered. The first is this: Does the Bible indicate that there will be apostasy in the church? The second is, What should be the Christian's attitude toward it?

There are five instances in the New Testament where religious apostasy is mentioned. The first is a proper apostasy from Judaism to Christ (Acts 21:21). The second warns of *the* apostasy which was not yet present when Paul wrote (II Thess. 2:3). The other three instances all use the verb "to depart" or "to apostatize" (Luke 8:13; I Tim. 4:1; Heb. 3: 12). Departure or apostasy can be from (1) the Word of God, (2) Christian doctrine, or (3) the living God, according to the three verb usages. Therefore, a definition of apostasy is this: A departure from truth previously accepted, involving the breaking of a professed relationship with God. Apostasy always involves willful leaving of previously known truth and embracing error.

Beyond any question, apostasy is both present and future in the church. It was present when Paul wrote to Timothy, and Paul looked forward to a future great apostasy distinctive enough to be labeled *the* apostasy. This present-future concept is similar to that of the present-future antichrist. There were antichrists present in the church in John's day and still he looked forward to *the* coming great Antichrist (I John 2: 18). Apostasy is something that plagues the church in every generation, though at the end of the Church age *the* great apostasy will come on the scene before the day of the Lord.

Dispensationalists, therefore, are not crying "Wolf" when they speak of the great apostasy or when they may see indications of apostasy in any generation. This is entirely Scriptural.

In I Timothy 4:1 Paul speaks of the apostasy in the "latter times," while he uses the phrase "in the last days" in II Timothy 3:1. Ellicott says that the difference between these phrases is this: the term "last days" points more specifically to the period immediately preceding the completion of the kingdom of Christ; the former only to a period future to the speaker. . . . In the apostasy of the present the inspired apostle sees the commencement of the fuller apostasy of the future."[23] Apostasy is both now and coming.

Dispensationalists usually connect the future apostasy with mystery Babylon of Revelation 17. Older commentators have referred Babylon to the evil world, making little distinction between the viewpoints of Revelation 17 and 18. The city with its commercial activities is the main emphasis in this view. Others have identified Babylon in Revelation 17 with Rome, that is, with the power of imperial Rome. This identification is based on the reference to the seven hills in 17:9. Since the time of the Reformation many commentators have identified Babylon with the papacy. Some do not restrict the identification to the papacy but rather see in Babylon of Revelation 17 apostate Christendom as a whole. This is the view of most dispensationalists, but it is not restricted to dispensationalists. Torrance, for instance, whose understanding of Babylon emphasizes the "evil world" aspect of it, nevertheless calls it "an imitation Kingdom of God, based on the demonic trinity."[24]

It is not necessary to identify mystery Babylon with the fu-

[23]C. J. Ellicott, *The Pastoral Epistles of St. Paul* (London: Longmans, 1864), p. 54.
[24]T. F. Torrance, *The Apocalypse Today* (Grand Rapids: Wm. B. Eerdmans Publishing Co., 1959), p. 115.

ture apostasy to prove that there will be a future apostasy. Other Scriptures show that without a doubt (II Thess. 2:3 and "last days" in II Tim. 3:1) . If Revelation 17 can also be identified with the future apostasy, this adds further details to an already revealed truth in Scripture. However many details one may or may not insist on in any identification of Revelation 17, it does seem clear that mystery Babylon, the mother of harlots, is a vast spiritual power so ecumenical or worldwide that it can enter effectively into league with the rulers and forces of the world, and so anti-God as to bend its force to persecute successfully the saints of God.

Thus the answer to the first question is clear: the Bible does definitely and clearly teach that there was, is, and will be apostasy in the professing church. The doctrine is not a figment of the dispensational imagination.

The second question is: What should be the true believer's attitude toward apostasy and apostates? There is no fixed formula that will answer the question. It goes without saying that in general he will abhor apostasy. However, what to do in the complex relationships of one's individual fellowship with other professed Christians is not a simple matter. In some relationships the servant of the Lord must in patience and gentleness seek to win the apostate from his error back to the truth (II Tim. 2:24-26) . In other cases apparently, apostates can go so far down the wrong road that the believer must avoid all contact with them, for, after describing the apostates of the last days, Paul clearly advises: "From such turn away" (II Tim. 3:5) . Actually there are two commands in this paragraph: (1) know that apostasy comes (v. 1) , and (2) turn away (v. 5) . To keep on realizing and turning away from such apostates, Paul says, is the only safe course of action. In other words, in some cases contact should be kept; in others, it should be broken. To be an ecclesiastical isolationist is wrong; never to be a separatist may be equally wrong, too. This is not to say that all the separatism that may in one way or another be linked to dispensational teaching is justified; but neither can antidispensationalists justify their emphasis that separatism is always wrong (I Cor. 11:19).

SUMMARY AND CONCLUSION

The principal emphasis of dispensationalism's doctrine of the Church is its understanding of the Church as distinctive in the purposes of God. Her character is distinct as a living organism, the Body of Christ. The time of her existence is distinctive to this present dispensation, which makes the Church distinct from Israel and not a new spiritual Israel. Dispensationalists recognize that the saving work of God today is being done in relation to the Church, and that there is a continuity which the redeemed of this dispensation share with the redeemed of other dispensations. Nevertheless, this does not make the Church a new Israel any more than those redeemed before Israel was called a nation could be called a "pre-old-Israel." The redeemed in the Body of Christ, the Church of this dispensation, are the continuation of the line of redeemed from other ages, but they form a distinct group in the heavenly Zion (Heb. 12:22-24).

While emphasizing the distinctiveness of the Church, the dispensationalist also recognizes certain relationships which the Church sustains. He does not say that there is no kingdom today, but insists that it is not the fulfillment of Old Testament kingdom promises. He does not imply that there were no redeemed in other ages. He recognizes believers in this age as a seed of Abraham but not the only seed. He seeks to be a realist concerning the course of this age and the Church's program in the midst of increasing apostasy. All his viewpoints stem from what he feels to be a consistent application of the literal principle of interpretation of Scripture.

If the dispensational emphasis on the distinctiveness of the

Church seems to result in a "dichotomy," let it stand as long as it is a result of literal interpretation. There is nothing wrong with God's having a purpose for Israel and a purpose for the Church and letting these two purposes stand together within His overall plan. After all, God has a purpose for angels which is different from His purpose for man. Yet no antidispensationalist worries about a "dichotomy" there. The unifying principle of Scripture is the glory of God as revealed in the variegated purposes revealed and yet to be revealed. To pick out one of these purposes and force everything else into its mold is to warp the revelation of God. This is the error of the nondispensationalist.

8

DISPENSATIONAL ESCHATOLOGY

ESCHATOLOGY is the study of future things, and it is through this area of Biblical studies that many have their first exposure to dispensational teaching. Because of this, some have consciously or unconsciously supposed that dispensationalism is primarily an outline (preferably on a chart) of the events of the future. While it is true that dispensational teaching and prophetic study have been interrelated in recent years especially, it was not always so.

Even opponents of dispensationalism realize that Darby's original dissatisfaction with the Church of England was not over the teaching of prophecy. His dissent was over the concept of the Church and his desire for more intimate fellowship with Christ which he felt was becoming increasingly impossible in the established system. In explaining why he left the church, he said:

> It was that I was looking for the body of CHRIST (which was not there, but perhaps in all the parish not one converted person) ; and collaterally, because I believed in a divinely appointed ministry. If Paul had come, he could not have preached (he had never been ordained) ; if a wicked ordained man, he had his title and must be recognized as a minister; the truest minister of Christ unordained could not. *It was a system contrary to what I found in Scripture.*[1]

[1]W. G. Turner, *John Nelson Darby* (London: C. A. Hammond, 1944), p. 18.

It was not until several years after leaving the Church of England that Darby became interested in prophecy and then through conferences at Powerscourt House out of which conferences the Irvingian movement grew. "Darbyism" was first a protest over the practice of the Established Church, not the propagating of a system of eschatology.

Likewise, there was little, if any, connection originally between dispensationalism and the earliest prophetic conference in America. It was called to counter postmillennial teaching and not to promote dispensationalism. If dispensational ideas were presented, they were incidental to the main purpose of the gathering. Nevertheless, this conference inevitably did promote dispensationalism because of the insistence on the absolute authority of the Scriptures, the literal fulfillment of Old Testament prophecy, and the expectation of the imminent coming of Christ.[2] But at the first the Plymouth Brethren did not appear. The leaders were denominational men.

In due time dispensationalism and a certain system of eschatology were wedded. But it was a *system* of eschatology, not merely an outline of future events. Indeed, it would be more accurate to call it a system of interpretation, for dispensational premillennialism not only includes a description of the future but also involves the meaning and significance of the entire Bible. It is not an alternate view of eschatology but a complete system of theology affecting many parts of the Bible other than Revelation 20.

THE FEATURES OF DISPENSATIONAL ESCHATOLOGY

What, then, are the salient features of dispensational premillennialism?

[2]Nathaniel West (ed.), *Premillennial Essays of the Prophetic Conference* (1878) (Chicago: Fleming H. Revell Co., 1879), p. 8.

A. THE HERMENEUTICAL PRINCIPLE

The hermeneutical principle is basic to the entire dispensational system including its eschatology. This affects everything, and, as we have tried to show in chapter 5, dispensationalism is the only system that practices the literal principle of interpretation consistently. Other systems practice literalism but not in every area of theology or on all parts of the Bible. For instance, in covenant premillennialism, which is antagonistic to dispensational premillennialism, literalism is abandoned at certain places in the Gospels. The Davidic, earthly kingdom is said not to be seen in the Gospels in Jesus' preaching. Ladd, for instance, declares that although the Jews understood Jesus to be offering the Davidic kingdom, in reality they misunderstood what He was saying, for according to Ladd's interpretation there is no literal earthly kingdom for Israel in view during the Gospels.[3] Consistent literalism is at the heart of dispensational eschatology.

B. FULFILLMENT OF OLD TESTAMENT PROPHECIES

The literal interpretation of Scripture leads naturally to a second feature—the literal fulfillment of Old Testament prophecies. This is the basic tenet of premillennial eschatology. If the prophecies of the Old Testament concerning the promises of the future made to Abraham and David are to be literally fulfilled, then there must be a future period, the millennium, in which they can be fulfilled, for the Church is not now fulfilling them in any literal sense. In other words, the literal picture of Old Testament prophecies demands either a future fulfillment or a nonliteral fulfillment. If they are to be fulfilled in the future, then the only time left for that fulfillment is the millennium. If they are not to be fulfilled literally, then the Church is the only kind of fulfillment they receive, but that is not a literal one. The amillen-

[3]George E. Ladd, *Crucial Questions About the Kingdom of God* (Grand Rapids: Wm. B. Eerdmans Publishing Co., 1952), pp. 112-114.

nialist says the latter; that is, that the fulfillment is in and by the Church. The covenant premillennialist says both; that is, the Church fulfills some of the prophecies, but there is a future millennial kingdom though it is not primarily for the purpose of fulfilling Israel's prophecies. The dispensational premillennialist says that the Church is in no way fulfilling these prophecies but that their fulfillment is reserved for the millennium and is one of the principal features of it.

C. A CLEAR DISTINCTION BETWEEN ISRAEL AND THE CHURCH

This understanding of the fulfillment of Old Testament prophecies quite naturally leads to a third feature—the clear distinction between Israel and the Church which is a vital part of dispensationalism. All other views bring the Church into Israel's fulfilled prophecies except dispensationalism. The amillenarian says that the Church completely fulfills Israel's prophecies, being the true, spiritual Israel. The covenant premillenarian sees the Church as fulfilling in some senses Israel's prophecies because both are the people of God while at the same time preserving the millennial age as a period of fulfillment too. The understanding of the how and when of the fulfillment of Israel's prophecies is in direct proportion to one's clarity of distinction between Israel and the Church.

D. PRETRIBULATION RAPTURE

The distinction between Israel and the Church leads to the belief that the Church will be taken from the earth before the beginning of the tribulation (which in one major sense concerns Israel). Pretribulationalism has become a part of dispensational eschatology. Originally this was due to the emphasis of the early writers and teachers on the imminency of the return of the Lord; more lately it has been connected with the dispensational conception of the distinctiveness of the Church. Amillennial eschatology, as far as the rapture is concerned, is posttribulational; covenant premillennialism is usually posttribulational also. Pretribulationalism has become a regular feature of dispensational premillennialism.

E. THE MILLENNIAL KINGDOM

Of course the thousand-year reign of Christ on the earth is also a feature of dispensational eschatology as it is of nondispensational premillennialism. The difference between the dispensational and nondispensational views of premillennialism is not in the fact of the coming millennial kingdom (for both include it in their systems) but in the integration of the kingdom into their overall systems. The doctrine of the millennial kingdom is for the dispensationalist an integral part of his entire scheme and interpretation of many Biblical passages. For the nondispensationalist the millennial kingdom is more like an addendum to his system. In representing the covenant premillennial viewpoint, Ladd has been justly criticized along these lines by another nondispensationalist who says that covenant premillennialism as represented by Ladd

> . . . is open to criticism not because of its premillennialism as such, but because it leaves the impression that the doctrine of the millennium is not sufficiently integrated into the author's overall view of the kingdom. Ladd's case for this doctrine rests solely upon two New Testament passages, Revelation 20:4-6 and I Corinthians 15:20-26, both hotly disputed. A firmer foundation might have been Old Testament prophecy. If merely the thousand-year duration were in question, then obviously Revelation 20 would be the only relevant text. But if the point at issue is the glorious reign of Messiah upon the earth, the renewal of nature, and the restoration of Israel, then the Old Testament is an important witness to this period and should not be neglected, even though prophetic perspective may not distinguish clearly among

church age, millennium, and eternal state. If there are
no Old Testament prophecies which demand a literal,
earthly fulfillment, then the purpose of the millennium
becomes partially obscure. In his effort to mediate, Ladd
will be criticized on one side for making the millennium
a mere appendix to his system, and on the other for re-
taining it at all![4]

Thus we may say that a millennial kingdom fully integrated
into the whole theological system is a feature of dispensational premillennialism.

These are the principal characteristics of dispensational
eschatology. Against these features of the dispensational
scheme certain objections have been raised and charges made.
Some of these charges against dispensational eschatology must
now be examined.

IS THE CROSS MINIMIZED?

A. THE CHARGE

A charge that is invariably leveled at dispensational eschatology is that the cross is minimized. It is related to the dispensationalist's teaching concerning the offer of the kingdom
to Israel when Christ was on earth. The objection goes something like this: You dispensationalists teach that when Christ
came to earth He offered Israel the Davidic kingdom promised in the Old Testament. But you do not answer the question, How could that offer be one which was made legiti-
mately and sincerely if Christ knew that He had to go to the
cross? If you still insist that it was a genuine offer, then you
have to admit the possibility that Israel could have accepted
the offer; and if they had, then the cross would have been
avoided and unnecessary. Antidispensationalist Mauro puts
it this way:

[4]J. Ramsey Michaels, Review of *The Gospel of the Kingdom*, by George
Eldon Ladd, *The Westminster Theological Journal*, 23 (November, 1960),
48.

> . . . when we press the vital question, what, in case the
> offer had been accepted, would have become of the
> Cross of Calvary and the atonement for the sins of the
> world, the best answer we get is that in that event,
> "atonement would have been made some other way."
> Think of it! "Some other way" than by the cross.[5]

Mauro does not document his supposed quote from dispensationalism. He puts words in the mouths of dispensationalists which they do not say. It is the answer he wants to try to force them to make, but it is a fabricated one.

Amillennialist Allis, who tries to force the same point, is more genteel in his manner:

> In other words, if the Jews had accepted the kingdom
> would there have been any place, any necessity for the
> cross? . . . the question raised by the Dispensational in-
> terpretation . . . amounts to this, Could men have been
> saved without the cross?[6]

More recently Bass voiced a similar objection.

> Such an extreme emphasis on the "postponed" kingdom,
> or even the "offered, but not set up" kingdom ultimately
> detracts from the glory of the church, which glory stems
> from the crucified and resurrected Christ.[7]

B. THE REPLY

It cannot be said too emphatically that dispensationalism has not taught and does not teach what is stated or implied in these quotations. The antidispensationalist's objection is based strictly and solely on what he hopes to be able to convince people that dispensationalists say, or on what he wishes they would say. *But it is not based on quotations from*

[5]Philip Mauro, *The Gospel of the Kingdom with an Examination of Modern Dispensationalism* (Boston: Hamilton Brothers, 1928), p. 23.
[6]Oswald T. Allis, *Prophecy and the Church* (Philadelphia: Presbyterian and Reformed Publishing Co., 1945), p. 75.
[7]Clarence B. Bass, *Backgrounds to Dispensationalism* (Grand Rapids: Wm. B. Eerdmans Publishing Co., 1960), p. 33.

dispensational writings. Dispensationalists do not say that the postponed kingdom concept makes the cross theoretically unnecessary or that it detracts from the glory of the Church. What we do say is the following:

> But, it will be asked, if the Davidic kingdom is post-
> poned that means that had it been received by the Jews
> it would not have been necessary for the Lord Jesus to
> have been crucified. The postponement of the kingdom
> is related primarily to the question of God's program
> in this age through the Church and not to the necessity
> of the crucifixion. The crucifixion would have been
> necessary as foundational to the establishment of the
> kingdom even if the Church age had never been con-
> ceived in the purposes of God. The question is not
> whether the crucifixion would have been avoided but
> whether the Davidic kingdom was postponed.[8]

There is no kingdom for Israel apart from the suffering Saviour as well as the reigning King. The crucifixion was as necessary to the establishing of the kingdom as it was to the building of the Church. The kingdom has a redemptive as well as a regal aspect. Chafer taught the same thing:

> But for the Church intercalation—which was wholly
> unforeseen and is wholly unrelated to any divine pur-
> pose which precedes it or which follows it—Israel would
> be expected to pass directly from the crucifixion to her
> kingdom; for it was not the death of Christ and His
> resurrection which demanded the postponement, but
> rather an unforeseen age.[9]

Notice well that Chafer did *not* say that Israel would have passed directly from receiving Christ's message to the king-dom, but he *did* say that they would have passed directly from

---

[8]Charles C. Ryrie, *Biblical Theology of the New Testament* (Chicago: Moody Press, 1959), p. 88.
[9]L. S. Chafer, *Systematic Theology* (Dallas: Seminary Press, 1947), V, 348-49.

the crucifixion to the kingdom had not the Church been included in God's program for the ages. One could scarcely ask for clearer statements of the dispensational position, and it is a position which in no way minimizes the cross and its place in relation to the Church and to the kingdom.

In addition to the clear avowals of dispensationalists, it is usually and rightly pointed out that this matter of a bona fide offer of the kingdom which God foreknew would be rejected is only one of several similar situations in the Bible. These involve that which is ultimately inscrutable, for example, the relation of the choice of man to the foreordained purposes of God. But even if we cannot fully understand or explain how there can be a genuine offer of the kingdom by the One who knew and planned that it would be rejected, we must not suggest that the offer was insincere. Chafer has pointed out similar situations in the Bible:

> With reference to other situations in which God's sovereign purpose seems for a time to depend on the free-will action of men, it will be remembered that God ordained a Lamb before the foundation of the world and that Lamb to be slain at God's appointed time and way. By so much it is made clear that God anticipated the sin of man and his great need of redemption. God, however, told Adam *not* to sin; yet if Adam had not sinned there would have been no need of that redemption which God had before determined as something to be wrought out. Was God uncertain whether He would save life on the earth until Noah consented to build an ark? Was the nation Israel a matter of divine doubt until Abraham manifested his willingness to walk with God? Was the birth of Christ dubiety until Mary assented to the divine plan respecting the virgin birth? ... Was the death of Christ in danger of being abortive and all the types and prophecies respecting His death of being proved untrue until Pilate made his decision re-

garding that death? . . . Could God promise a kingdom
on the earth knowing and so planning that it would be
rejected in the first advent but realized in the second
advent? Could God offer a kingdom in the first advent
in sincerity, knowing and determining that it would
not be established until the second advent?[10]

Such illustrations put the sincere offer of the kingdom and
its preplanned rejection in its proper perspective and should
keep one from running to illogical conclusions as the nondispensationalist does. It is particularly astounding that a Cal-
vinist like Allis should stumble at this matter when he would
not even suggest questioning the sincerity of God in offering
salvation to nonelect people. One may grant that in the final
analysis such matters are inexplicable, but one does not need
to charge God with insincerity.

To sum up: The cross is in no way minimized by the
teaching of the postponement of the kingdom.[11] The postponement relates to the outworking of God's purpose in the
Church, the Body of Christ, and certainly the cross is central
to this work of God. Further, even if there had been no
Church as a part of God's program, the cross was necessary to
the establishing of the Messianic kingdom. In both purposes
of God—the Church and the kingdom—the cross is basic.
This is the teaching of dispensationalism and, instead of minimizing the cross of Christ, it magnifies it.

[10]*Ibid.*, V, 347-48.
[11]One readily admits that the dispensational concept concerning the offer
and rejection of the kingdom at the first advent of Christ is inadequately
described by the word *postponed*. It is a word which views the matter from
a human standpoint and in relation to the kingdom program for Israel only.
From the divine perspective, of course, nothing is ever postponed, for all
events are taking place according to God's perfectly preplanned order and
right on schedule. Too, from God's viewpoint the fulfillment of Israel's
promised kingdom was never scheduled until the second advent though it
was offered at the first advent. The word *postponed* is justified only from
the human viewpoint and only in relation to the kingdom purpose. Nevertheless its use does have justification, and it has been found helpful in
conveying the idea involved. Though one could wish for a more inclusive
word, there does not seem to be sufficient reason for rejecting it completely.

C. TURNING THE TABLES

Let us suppose for sake of discussion that the dispensational interpretation of Jesus' offer of the Davidic kingdom in the Gospels is not correct. If He was not preaching about the millennial kingdom when He said, "Repent: for the kingdom of heaven is at hand" (Matt. 4:17), then He must have been talking about a spiritual kingdom in the hearts of men (for there are no other choices). This is, of course, the kind of kingdom which both the amillennialist and the covenant premillennialist say Jesus was offering in the Gospels. Ladd, for instance, says:

> . . . Jesus did not offer to the Jews the earthly kingdom any more than he offered himself to them as their glorious earthly king. . . . God's kingdom was first to come to men in a spiritual sense, as the Saviour-King comes in meekness to suffer and die, defeating Satan and bringing into the sphere of God's kingdom a host of people who are redeemed from the kingdom of Satan and of sin; and subsequently it is to be manifested in power and glory as the King returns to judge and reign.[12]

Allis, representing the amillennial view, holds the same viewpoint about the kingdom offered in the Gospels (although Allis would not agree with Ladd in seeing a future reign on earth for Messiah). Allis says:

> What was the nature of the kingdom which they [John the Baptist and Jesus] announced? . . . The kingdom announced by John and by Jesus was primarily and essentially a moral and spiritual kingdom. It was to be prepared for by repentance. . . . It was to be entered by a new birth. . . . Such passages as the above indicate with unmistakable plainness that from the very outset Jesus not merely gave no encouragement to, but defi-

[12]Ladd, *op. cit.*, p. 114.

nitely opposed, the expectation of the Jews that an earthly, Jewish kingdom of glory, such as David had established centuries before, was about to be set up.[13]

Very clearly, the amillennialist and the covenant premillennialist both agree that Jesus was not offering the earthly, Davidic kingdom during His earthly ministry. Instead, they say, He was offering a spiritual kingdom. Futhermore, the condition for receiving that spiritual kingdom, Allis says, was repentance and the new birth. Both the repentance and new birth Allis is talking about were the subject of Jesus' teaching *before* the cross. Therefore, the dispensationalist might turn the tables on the amillennialist and the covenant premillennialist and ask two questions similar to those which he is often asked.

. The first is this: If the Jews living during the earthly ministry of Jesus had received His teaching and had repented and been born again, does this mean there was in those days a way of salvation which was different from salvation through the death of Christ? It seems as if it would mean this, and one would be forced to conclude that the amillennialist and the covenant premillennialist teach more than one way of salvation.

The second question is this: If the Jews had received this spiritual kingdom and had been saved, then does this not mean that the cross might have been unnecessary? If the Jews had immediately accepted the spiritual kingdom Jesus offered, then what would have happened to the cross?

Without doubt the amillennialist and the covenant premillennialist would reply to both these questions that they are theoretical and do not demand an answer. They view the whole plan of God from a strictly human viewpoint and are therefore not entirely fair questions. And with such a reply from the amillennialist and covenant premillennialist the

[13]Allis, *op. cit.*, pp. 69-71.

dispensationalist would agree. These are foolish questions. Perhaps the same is true of the similar questions asked of dispensationalists.

IS THE KINGDOM DESPIRITUALIZED?

A. THE CHARGE

A second objection always raised about dispensational eschatology is that it makes the doctrine of the kingdom so materialistic that it is unscriptural. It is said that dispensationalists despiritualize the kingdom with their materialistic notions of the political and earthly reign of Christ. The charge assumes that materialistic is the opposite of spiritual, and since the millennial kingdom is earthly it is materialistic and therefore cannot be spiritual.

B. THE BASIS FOR THE CHARGE

There are probably two reasons why this charge against dispensationalism persists. One is that dispensationalists have undoubtedly emphasized the millennial kingdom and its relation to the fulfillment of Israel's promises almost to the point of neglecting other aspects of the doctrine. The emphasis on the millennial kingdom has had a tendency to place in the background truth concerning the eternal kingdom of God. Emphasis on the relation of the millennial kingdom to the nation Israel has perhaps led to a spotlighting of the aspects of the earthly glory of that kingdom which has been construed as emphasizing exclusively its material aspects. The very fact that the millennial kingdom is earthly lends itself to a highlighting of the material aspects of that kingdom.

While the emphasis on the millennial kingdom might be called by some an overemphasis, it was a natural one which grew out of the lack of any teaching on the subject in the days in which dispensationalism began to flourish. This is not to say that it was a new truth discovered by Darby in Britain and by the participants in the prophetic conferences in America, but it was a truth which was brought to light again at that time and given the natural emphasis of any rediscovery. Though this does not necessarily excuse any erroneous overemphasis, it may explain it.

A second reason on which the charge of despiritualizing the kingdom is based is the alleged dispensational distinction between the kingdom of God and the kingdom of Heaven. Dispensationalists are said to distinguish rigidly between these two phrases so that the kingdom of God is the eternal spiritual kingdom and the kingdom of Heaven is the millennial earthly kingdom. The kingdom of Heaven, or the millennial kingdom, was usually given the more thorough treatment in dispensational writings. For instance, the Old Testament note on the kingdom in the Scofield Reference Bible is given over almost entirely to the theocratic kingdom.[14] The New Testament note discusses exclusively the Davidic kingdom,[15] although in another place there is a note on the differences between the kingdom of God and the kingdom of Heaven which does include facts about the eternal kingdom.[16] Similar distinction and emphasis are found in Chafer's summary discussion of the kingdom in which he devotes two lines to the kingdom of God and more than a page to the Davidic, millennial kingdom.[17]

This kind of emphasis based upon the kingdom-of-heaven—kingdom-of-God distinction has been typical of dispensational writers and gives rise to the charge. Particularly do nondispensationalists like to attempt to show that the phrase *kingdom of heaven* cannot refer exclusively to the millennial kingdom. And therefore to make it so refer—as dispensationalists allegedly do—is to despiritualize the kingdom.

[14]Pp. 976-77.
[15]Pp. 1226-27.
[16]P. 1003.
[17]Chafer, *Systematic Theology*, VII, 223-24.

C. DISPENSATIONAL TEACHING CONCERNING THE KINGDOM OF HEAVEN AND THE KINGDOM OF GOD

As implied above, the nondispensationalist tries to build his case against dispensationalism on the dispensationalist's supposed distinction between the kingdom of Heaven and the kingdom of God. For instance, Ladd says flatly that "the dispensational position is maintained on the basis of the distinction between the Kingdom of God and the Kingdom of heaven."[18] It is true that dispensationalists have sometimes pinned the label "kingdom of Heaven" to the earthly, millennial kingdom and the label "kingdom of God" to the eternal, spiritual kingdom. However, the antidispensationalist has created a straw man by insisting that the entire position is maintained on the basis of a distinction of this sort. Within the ranks of dispensationalists there are those who hold to the distinction and those who do not.[19] This is not at all determinative. John F. Walvoord has shown this very clearly in his review of Ladd's book *Crucial Questions About the Kingdom of God.* He says:

> Another major confusion in this discussion is the mistaken notion commonly held by nondispensationalists that the distinction often affirmed between the kingdom of God and the kingdom of heaven is essential to the dispensational argument. Actually one could maintain this distinction and be an amillenarian or deny it and be a dispensationalist. The distinction as usually presented is between the kingdom of heaven as an outward sphere of profession and the kingdom of God as a sphere of reality including only the elect. . . . As far as affecting the premillennial or dispensational argument, in the opinion of the reviewer it is irrelevant.

---

[18]Ladd, *op. cit.,* p. 106.

[19]Erich Sauer (*The Triumph of the Crucified*) and Alva J. McClain (*The Greatness of the Kingdom*) do not maintain a distinction, and both men are recognized dispensationalists.

The issue is not whether the kingdom of heaven is postponed but whether the Messianic kingdom offered by the Old Testament prophets and expected by the Jewish people in connection with the first advent was offered, rejected, and postponed until the second advent. We believe the author is therefore incorrect in building the dispensational doctrine of a postponed kingdom on the distinction between the kingdom of God and the kingdom of heaven. It depends rather upon the distinction between the present form of the kingdom and the future form of the kingdom, which is entirely a different matter.[20]

In other words, the issue is not the labels but the present form of the kingdom. If it is the Church, then dispensationalism is unwarranted. If the present form of the kingdom is not the Church and if the future form is the Davidic kingdom on earth, then dispensational premillennialism is the only answer.

Whether the kingdom in present form is the Church or whether during this age the Davidic theocratic kingdom has been postponed depends on one's view of the kingdom preached by Jesus. Although Bass disagrees with the postponed kingdom idea, he states the crux of the matter clearly when he says:

The postponed-kingdom idea grows out of the basic concept of what the kingdom was to be, and what it shall yet be. This is held [by dispensationalism] to be a literal restoration of the national kingdom, and since no such covenanted kingdom with the Davidic throne has appeared, it must have been postponed. The kingdom and the church can in no way be paralleled in the plan of God.[21]

[20]John F. Walvoord, Review of *Crucial Questions About the Kingdom of God*, by George Eldon Ladd, *Bibliotheca Sacra*, 110 (January, 1953), 6.
[21]Bass, *op. cit.*, p. 32.

In Bass' nondispensational view the kingdom in present form
is the Church—"the recipient of the covenantal relation with
God"[22]—and because Israel rejected Christ "the 'spiritual
Israel' in the form of the church was instituted."[23] But if one's
basic concept of the kingdom is a spiritual one, then the
Church can easily be assumed to be the form of the kingdom
today. If Jesus preached and offered the Davidic kingdom,
then, as Bass rightly declares, it was obviously postponed, for
it simply has not been established according to the picture of
the Old Testament promises.

Although dispensationalists insist that the kingdom Jesus
preached was the Davidic kingdom and that the establishing
of the Church is not the fulfillment of it, they do not fail to
recognize the presence of the universal and spiritual kingdom
or rule of God. This existed before the promises of any other
distinct form of a kingdom were ever given to David. God's
sovereignty over the entire creation is recognized in many
Old Testament passages (Ps. 10:16; 103:19; 59:13; Dan. 4:34-
35). Even though there has been a great deal of rebellion in
the earth, God still rules His universe.

In addition, there is a spiritual aspect to God's kingdom
rule. It is not a separate kingdom from His universal reign,
but it is a sphere within that in which He rules the hearts and
lives of those who trust Him. Believers in this age have been
brought into the kingdom of His dear Son (Col. 1:13), and
believers in every age are part of this spiritual kingdom. But
the spiritual feature of this present age is not revealed in terms
of a kingdom but in the Church, the Body of Christ. Even
during the millennium there will be those who are in the
Davidic kingdom but not in any spiritual kingdom, simply
because they live under the government of Christ yet do not
receive Him into their hearts.

The promises to David also concerned the rule of God on

[22]*Ibid.*, p. 30.
[23]*Ibid.*

the earth and in the hearts of men, but with certain other distinct details which made David understand some kingdom other than the general rule of God. It was this Davidic kingdom which Jesus offered and not the general rule of God over the earth or His spiritual reign in individual lives. If it were the spiritual kingdom Christ was offering, then "such an announcement would have had no special significance whatever to Israel, for such a rule of God has *always* been recognized among the people of God."[24] The kingdom the Lord preached was something different from either the general rule of God in His overall sovereignty or the rule of God in the individual heart. Therefore, when a dispensationalist says that the kingdom is postponed, he is speaking of the Davidic kingdom, but he also affirms the continuing presence of the universal kingdom and the spiritual rule of God in individual hearts today. God does not rule in only one way or through only one means. Even the amillennialist recognizes the universal kingdom and the Israelitish kingdom of the Old Testament. The covenant premillennialist includes in addition the millennial kingdom. The dispensationalist recognizes all of these various ways in which God has ruled, but keeps distinct the Church as another purpose of God in addition to His kingdom purposes. The antidispensationalist will not allow the dispensationalist to maintain this last distinction though he himself maintains others even within the general subject of the kingdom!

This discussion started with the matter of a distinction between the phrases *kingdom of heaven* and *kingdom of God*. This distinction is not the issue at all. The issue is whether or not the Church is the kingdom, and the distinctiveness of the Church in this age as recognized by dispensationalists is a *sine qua non* of the system. One sees again how the ecclesiology and eschatology of dispensationalism are closely related.

[24]Alva J. McClain, *The Greatness of the Kingdom* (Grand Rapids: Zondervan Publishing House, 1959), p. 303.

D. Dispensational Teaching Concerning the Spiritual Character of the Millennial Kingdom

Can dispensationalism be properly charged with envisioning the Davidic kingdom as "material" and "carnal"? The answer is emphatically no. To do this is to misrepresent dispensationalism grossly. Simply because the kingdom is on the earth does not mean that it cannot be spiritual. If that were so, then no living Christian could be spiritual either, for he is very much a resident of the earth. Neither is it necessary to spiritualize the earthly kingdom in order to have a spiritual kingdom. If that were so, then again no Christian could be spiritual until he is spiritualized! The contrast is not between "materialistic" and "spiritual," but between the presence and absence of the King on this earth.

This charge against premillennialism (for it is really not distinctive to dispensationalism) is not new. Peters countered it in his day and contemporary writers are doing it today.[25] So much has been written concerning the spiritual character of the millennium by dispensationalists that it seems unnecessary to reproduce the same facts here. If anything is obvious from the literal interpretation of passages concerning the millennial kingdom, it is that the period will be a rule of God which includes the highest ideals of spirituality. Righteousness is the descriptive word for that time. Holiness, truth, justice, glory and the fullness of the Spirit are all used in the Scriptures to characterize the kingdom on earth. McClain and Sauer both devote many pages in their respective books to the spiritual characteristics of the millennial kingdom.[26, 27] It is a time when God harmoniously joins the spiritual and the

[25]George N. H. Peters, *The Theocratic Kingdom* (Grand Rapids: Kregel Publications, 1952), III, 460. The work was originally published in 1884. Cf. J. D. Pentecost, *Things to Come* (Findlay, Ohio: Dunham Publishing Co., 1958), pp. 482-87.

[26]McClain, *op. cit.*, pp. 519-26.

[27]Erich Sauer, *From Eternity to Eternity* (London: Paternoster Press, 1954), pp. 143-44, 157-61.

earthly in a final display of the glory of the King *on* this earth.

A humorous illustration from McClain will serve as a fitting conclusion to this discussion of the charge that dispensationalism despiritualizes the kingdom.

> During a church banquet a group of preachers were discussing the nature of the Kingdom of God. One expressed his adherence to the premillennial view of a literal kingdom. . . . To this a rather belligerent two-hundred-pound preacher snorted, "Ridiculous! Such an idea is nothing but materialism." When asked to state his own view, he replied, "The Kingdom is a *spiritual* matter. The Kingdom of God has *already* been established, and is *within* you. Don't you gentlemen know that the Kingdom is not eating and drinking, but righteousness and peace and joy in the Holy Ghost?" And the speaker reached hungrily across the table and speared another enormous piece of fried chicken! . . . At the risk of being thought tiresome, let me recite the obvious conclusion: If the Kingdom of God can exist now on earth in a two-hundred-pound preacher full of fried chicken, without any reprehensible materialistic connotations, perhaps it could also exist in the same way among men on earth who will at times be eating and drinking under more perfect conditions in a future millennial kingdom.[28]

Dispensational eschatology in no way minimizes the cross or despiritualizes the millennial kingdom. The contingent offer of the Davidic kingdom by Jesus was bona fide, and it was not a spiritual kingdom which He announced. This does not mean that dispensationalists fail to recognize the rule of God in the heart today, but the body of believers today constitute the Church, not the kingdom. The alleged stand-or-fall distinction between the kingdom of Heaven and kingdom

[28]McClain, *op. cit.*, pp. 519-20.

of God is not an issue at all. All shades of theological thought recognize different kingdoms or different aspects of the rule of God. What labels are attached to them is a minor matter. The question is whether the Church is recognized as a distinct purpose of God today, and whether or not a place is given for the literal fulfillment of the Davidic, earthly, and spiritual kingdom in the future millennium. The recognition of the distinctiveness of the Church and consistently literal interpretation of Israel's promises are the bases of a dispensational eschatology.

9

COVENANT THEOLOGY

THROUGHOUT THIS BOOK reference has been made many times to covenant theology. Many of its features and characteristics have been noted and discussed, but the subject has nowhere been systematized. At this point there is, therefore, a need for systematizing and emphasizing some aspects of covenant theology.

DEFINITION OF COVENANT THEOLOGY

Formal definitions of covenant theology are not easy to find even in the writings of covenant theologians. Most of the statements which pass for definitions are in fact descriptions or characterizations of the system. The article in *Baker's Dictionary of Theology* comes close to a definition when it says that covenant theology is distinguished by "the place it gives to the covenants" because it "represents the whole of Scripture as being covered by covenants: (1) the covenant of works, and (2) the covenant of grace."[1] This is a fair description and possibly a definition. Covenant theology, then, is a system of theology based upon the two covenants of works and of grace as governing categories for the understanding of the entire Bible.

In covenant theology the covenant of works is said to be agreement between God and Adam promising life to Adam for perfect obedience and including death as the penalty for

[1]George N. M. Collins (minister in Edinburgh, Scotland), "Covenant Theology," *Baker's Dictionary of Theology* (Grand Rapids: Baker Book House, 1960), p. 144.

failure. But Adam sinned and thus man failed to meet the requirements of the covenant of works. Therefore a second covenant, the covenant of grace, was brought into operation. Berkhof defines it as "that gracious agreement between the offended God and the offending but elect sinner, in which God promises salvation through faith in Christ, and the sinner accepts this believingly, promising a life of faith and obedience."[2]

Some Reformed theologians have introduced a third covenant, the covenant of redemption. It was made in eternity past and became the basis for the covenant of grace, just described, between God and the elect. This covenant of redemption is supposed to be "the agreement between the Father, giving the Son as Head and Redeemer of the elect, and the Son, voluntarily taking the place of those whom the Father had given him."[3]

These two or three covenants become the core and basis of operation for covenant theology in its interpretation of the Scriptures. Thus the theological system which makes these so-called theological covenants its base is covenant theology.

HISTORY OF COVENANT THEOLOGY

We should remind ourselves again that the antiquity of a doctrine does not prove its truth nor does the recency of a doctrine prove its falsehood. Bear, a covenant theologian, rightly said in an article against dispensationalism:

> Of course, doctrines may be new and yet not untrue. We believe that the Holy Spirit can lead the Church into new apprehensions of truth. Again, a doctrine may be new in the sense that it is the further development of a previously held doctrine, or it may be new in the sense that it contradicts the previously held views. Even

[2]Louis Berkhof, *Systematic Theology* (Grand Rapids: Wm. B. Eerdmans Publishing Co., 1941), p. 277.
[3]*Ibid.*, p. 271.

in the latter case it may not be untrue, but certainly its validity must be subjected to a much more searching scrutiny.[4]

In the next section we will examine the Scriptural support offered for covenant theology, but in the meantime it is not entirely irrelevant to survey the history of the development of what has come to be known as covenant theology. After all, nearly every antidispensational writer attempts to make something of the relative recency of systematized dispensationalism. Those who are of the Reformed tradition always attempt to imply that dispensationalism is a mere infant compared to the ancient and wise man of covenant theology. Let us examine the "antiquity" of covenant theology; the causes for its development; and the refinements, if any, that have come into the original system.

Systematized covenant theology is recent.[5] It was not the expressed doctrine of the early church. It was never taught by church leaders in the Middle Ages. It was not even mentioned by the primary leaders of the Reformation. Indeed, covenant theology as a system is not any older than dispensationalism is. This does not mean it is not Biblical, but it does dispel the notion that covenant theology has been throughout all church history the ancient guardian of the truth which is only recently being sniped at by dispensationalism. There were no references to covenant theology in any of the great confessions of faith until the Westminster Confession in 1647, and even in that confession covenant theology was not as fully developed as it was later by Reformed theologians.

The covenant (or federal) theory arose sporadically and apparently independently late in the sixteenth century. The

[4]James E. Bear, *Dispensationalism and the Covenant of Grace* (Richmond: Union Seminary Review, 1938), p. 4.
[5]Cornelius Van Til, a covenant theologian, affirms this: "The idea of covenant theology has only in modern times been broadly conceived" ("Covenant Theology," *Twentieth Century Encyclopedia* [Grand Rapids: Baker Book House, 1955], I, 306).

first proponents of the covenant view were reformers who were against the strict predestinarianism of the reformers of Switzerland and France. Covenant theology does not appear in the writings of Luther, Zwingli, Calvin or Melanchthon, even though they discussed at length the related doctrines of sin, depravity, redemption, etc. They had every opportunity to incorporate the covenant idea, but they did not. It is true that Calvin, for instance, spoke of the continuity of redemptive revelation and of the idea of a covenant between God and His people, but this was not covenant theology. The only way covenant theology can be discovered in the major reformers is to do what one covenant theologian does, not restrict the term "covenant theology" to "the more fully developed covenant theology of the seventeenth century."[6] But, of course, dispensationalists would never be allowed to point to any kind of undeveloped dispensationalism in any thinker before Darby!

The earliest traces of the covenant or federal idea are found in secondary reformers like Andrew Hyperius (1511-1564), Kaspar Olevianus (1536-1587), and Rafael Eglinus (1559-1622). William Ames (1576-1633), who ministered in England and Holland and was a teacher of Cocceius, taught the covenant of works. Up to the time of Johannes Cocceius (1603-1669) any teaching of covenant theology was not widespread and its exponents were men whose influence was definitely secondary to the great reformers of the time and who were protesting the strict predestinarianism of those reformers.[7]

Cocceius was a German who was influenced by the teaching of Melanchthon. His training was in the less strict school of thought concerning predestination. As a teacher in Holland he was much concerned about the problems of Arminian-

---

[6]John Murray, *The Covenant of Grace* (London: Tyndale Press, 1954), p. 3.

[7]W. Adams Brown, "Covenant Theology," *Encyclopedia of Religion and Ethics* (Edinburgh: Clark, 1935), IV, 220-22.

ism on the one hand and the harsh ways of the rigorous Calvinists on the other hand. He wanted to find a way to take theology back to the Bible and find its doctrines there rather than in the teachings of the strict Calvinism of his day. He was definitely of the Reformed group, but desirous, along with others, of finding some way to blunt the sharp and highly debated views on predestination current in his day.

> The great aim of his life was to lead theology back to the Bible, as its only living source, and to supply it with a vital foundation, gathered from the Bible itself. He believed that he found such a basis in the idea of a twofold covenant of God with man (*foedus naturale,* BEFORE, and *foedus gratia,* AFTER the fall). Thus he became the author of the federal theology, which made the historical development of the Revelation the ruling principle of theological inquiry, and of theology as a system, and thus became the founder of a purely biblical theology (as a history of Redemption). He adhered as closely as possible to predestinarian theology, but it was only a mechanical adhesion. It is not the idea of *election of grace,* but of a guidance of grace, which predominates in his whole system.[8]

Cocceius set forth his views in a work published in 1648. (Poiret's systematic work on dispensationalism was dated 1687.) In it Cocceius expounded the concept of two covenants, the covenants of works and of grace. In both, he said, man had a part to play and a responsibility to meet. He made these covenants the basis, background, and substance of all God's dealings with man for his redemption. Thus Cocceius' contribution was a detailing and systematizing of the idea of the covenants, giving a more prominent part to man in contrast to the rigorous predestinarianism of his day, and making the covenant idea the governing category of all Scripture.

[8]John Henry Kurtz, *Text Book of Church History* (Philadelphia: J. B. Lippincott Co., 1888), II, 213.

Cocceius, though the systematizer of covenant theology, was not entirely the father of it. Not only were some of the ideas of covenant theology found in earlier writers as indicated above, but also the Westminster Confession's covenant of works and covenant of grace appeared one year before the publication of Cocceius' work on the subject. In the Westminster Confession the covenants are used more in the nature of general divisions of the purpose of God; in Cocceius the covenant idea received "an extension and systematic development which raised it to a place of importance in theology it had not formerly possessed. It not only is made by him the leading idea of his system . . . but in his treatment the whole development of sacred history is governed by this thought."[9]

But whatever good Cocceius' work had done in countering the excesses of the Calvinism of his day was short-lived. Herman Witsius (1636-1708) was mainly responsible for extending the covenant of grace concept back into eternity. He paralleled the covenant idea with the decrees and extreme predestinarian position against which Cocceius was protesting. The Cocceian party repudiated Witsius' views, but they gained acceptance among subsequent covenant theologians.

The linking of the covenant of grace with the eternal decrees led some to introduce the third covenant of redemption made in eternity past between the persons of the Godhead as the basis for the covenant of grace. But this was a later development of the covenant scheme and is not in Cocceius and the Westminster Confession.

Covenant theology came to America with the Puritans through the writings of Francis Turretin and Herman Witsius, and was championed in the new world in the works of John Cotton and others. However, although the idea of the Covenant of Grace was often referred to, there was no agreement on the practical aspects of the doctrine, especially the position

---

[9]James Orr, *The Progress of Dogma* (Grand Rapids: Wm. B. Eerdmans Publishing Co.), pp. 302-3.

of children. This gave rise to the Half-way Covenant, Stoddardeanism, compromising practices in the churches, and a shift from a substitutionary view of the atonement to governmental and moral theories. Opposition to these unorthodox ideas and a reappearance of covenant theology came in the writings of Charles and A. A. Hodge of Princeton.[10]

To sum up: covenant theology is a post-Reformation development in doctrine. It began as a reaction to extreme Calvinism, but was soon twisted back to be the handmaid of Calvinism. The covenant statement in the Westminster Confession is undeveloped; it was Cocceius who developed the idea and Witsius who made it a governing category of Scriptural interpretation. But covenant theology as taught today is a development from both the theology of the Reformers (who did not teach a covenant scheme at all) and the teachings of Cocceius and the Westminster Confession. Covenant theology is not the theology of the Reformers; covenant theology is not today the same as it was when originally introduced. Covenant theology is a refinement— and the refining did not antedate Darby by many years. Covenant theology cannot claim much more antiquity than dispensationalism, and in its present form it is considerably refined. If lack of antiquity is detrimental and refinement is disallowed for dispensationalism, then by the same two criteria covenant theology is discredited. And if these matters are basically nonessential for covenant theology, then they are likewise irrelevant in the critique of dispensationalism.

BIBLICAL BASIS FOR COVENANT THEOLOGY

The ideas contained in the covenants of works and grace are certainly not unscriptural.[11] But they are not ideas which

[10]See Peter Y. De Jong, *The Covenant Idea in New England Theology* (Grand Rapids: Wm. B. Eerdmans Publishing Co., 1945), pp. 87-191.
[11]Even Chafer said of the covenant of redemption: "This covenant rests upon but slight revelation. It is rather sustained largely by the fact that it seems both reasonable and inevitable." L. S. Chafer (*Systematic Theology* [Dallas: Seminary Press], I, 42).

are systematized and formalized by Scripture into covenants. At least the dispensationalist finds the word *dispensation* used of one or two of his specific dispensations (Eph. 1:10; 3:9) ; the covenant theologian *never* finds in the Bible the term "covenant of works" or "covenant of grace." This does not prove that the concepts are not warranted, but it ought to make a covenant theologian go slow before he makes rash charges against dispensationalists for using the term *dispensation*. If the dispensationalist is in error in this regard, the covenant theologian is in gross error!

Nevertheless, the question is, What is the Scriptural proof for the covenant of works and the covenant of grace? One of Allis' most recent essays was on the covenant of works. This is what he wrote concerning the Scriptural basis for the covenant of works:

> The relationship established in Eden has been properly called the covenant of works. That it promised life as the reward for obedience is not immediately stated. But it is made abundantly clear elsewhere, notably in Deuteronomy. The First Psalm is a poetical expounding of this covenant, and it has its counterpart in Romans 2:7-9.[12]

The passages from Deuteronomy which he cites in a footnote are 6:5, 10-12ff.; 30:15-20. They have to do with life *in the promised land,* not in Heaven.

His proof for the covenant of grace is this:

> This covenant is first set forth cryptically in the words of the protevangel [Gen. 3:15], which promised Eve ultimate triumph over the enemy of her race. In this covenant, the emphasis is on faith. This is made clear in the wonderful words that are said of Abram: "And he believed in the Lord, and he accounted it to him for righteousness," to which Paul appeals to show that

[12]Oswald T. Allis, "The Covenant of Works," *Basic Christian Doctrines,* ed. Carl F. H. Henry (New York: Holt, Rinehart, and Winston, 1962), p. 97.

Abraham was justified by faith and not by the works of the law.[13]

An older writer, Hodge, presents this as his first (of seven) Scriptural proofs for the covenant of grace:

> As shown at the opening of this chapter such a Covenant is virtually implied in the existence of an eternal Plan of salvation mutually formed by and to be executed by three Persons.[14]

His further proofs include John 17; Isaiah 53:10-11; John 10: 18; Luke 22:29.

The point of this is not to be able to conclude that these covenants are unscriptural, but simply to show that they are deductions, not inductions, from Scripture. The existence of the covenants is not found by an inductive examination of passages; it is a conclusion deduced from certain Scriptural evidence. Now, if it is permissible for the covenant theologian to base his entire system on a deduction rather than a clear statement of Scripture, why can he not permit the dispensationalist to deduce the existence of various dispensations, especially when certain of the dispensations are specifically named in Scripture? The dispensationalist has more inductive evidence for the existence of the specific dispensations than does the covenant theologian for his covenants of works and grace; and the dispensationalist has as much, if not more, right to deduce his dispensational scheme as does the covenant theologian his covenant scheme.

What the covenant theologian does to make up for the lack of specific Scriptural support for the covenants of works and grace is to project the general idea of covenant in the Bible and the specific covenants (like the covenant with Abraham)

---

[13]*Ibid.*
[14]A. A. Hodge, *Outlines of Theology* (Grand Rapids: Wm. B. Eerdmans Publishing Co., 1928), p. 371.

into these covenants of works and grace.[15] No one disputes the fact that covenant is a very basic idea in Scripture and that a number of specific covenants are revealed in Scripture. But there remains still the stark reality that nowhere does Scripture speak of a covenant of works or a covenant of grace as it speaks of a covenant with Abraham or a covenant at Sinai or the new covenant.

Seeking to support a revelation of the covenant of grace from Genesis 3:15, Payne cites as proof: "Genesis 3:15 is, in fact, not even called a *b'rith;* but it is necessarily assumed to be so, both because of the presence of all the important features and because of the development of all subsequent redemptive *b'riths* from it." In the preceding sentence he states that those covenant features which are supposedly present in Genesis 3:15 are there only "in a most rudimentary form."[16] Allis calls the revelation of this important covenant in Genesis 3:15 cryptic and Payne says it was rudimentary. This is all very strange and hard to swallow, especially when the Biblical covenants with Abraham, Israel, David, and others are so clearly and specifically revealed. Abraham had no doubt that a covenant was being made when God Himself passed between the pieces of the sacrifice (Gen. 15:17-21). And yet we are asked to believe in the existence of a covenant of grace which was scarcely revealed, although it is the fountainhead out of which even the Abrahamic covenant came!

In another recent article on the covenant of grace there are Scripture references in the author's discussion of (1) the covenant with Abraham, (2) the covenant on Sinai, (3) further covenants like the Davidic, and (4) the New Testament culmination; but there is *not one* reference from Scripture in his several sections which deals directly with the establishing of the covenant of grace or its characteristics. There are

[15]As Murray does in *The Covenant of Grace.*
[16]J. Barton Payne, *The Theology of the Older Testament* (Grand Rapids: Zondervan Publishing House, 1962), p. 92.

references concerning the blessings of salvation, but none to support the covenant of grace.[17] That which is missing is rather significant and revealing.

THE HERMENEUTICS OF COVENANT THEOLOGY

Something has already been said in chapter 5 on the hermeneutical basis of dispensationalism and covenant theology. There is no need to repeat here. Only two points concern us at this juncture.

The first is this: as a result of the covenant of grace idea, covenant theology has been forced to place as its most basic principle of interpretation the principle of interpreting the Old Testament by the New. So Berkhof writes: ". . . the main guide to the interpretation of the Old Testament is certainly to be found in the New."[18] Ladd, though disclaiming the label of a covenant theologian, declares: "The present writer is ready to agree with the amillennialist that there is only one place to find a hermeneutic: in the New Testament."[19]

Of course there is everything right about letting the New Testament guide us in our understanding of the Old Testament, but there is everything wrong about imposing the New Testament on the Old. And this is exactly what the covenant theologian does under the guise of a basic hermeneutical principle which is allowable only if rightly used. The covenant theologian in his zeal to make Christ all in all is guilty of superimposing Him arbitrarily on the Old Testament. He does the same with the doctrine of the Church and with the concept of salvation through faith in Christ.

The second point is this: as a result of this forced category

[17]Herbert M. Carson, "The Covenant of Grace," *Basic Christian Doctrines,* ed. Carl F. H. Henry (New York: Holt, Rinehart, and Winston, 1962), pp. 117-23.
[18]Louis Berkhof, *Principles of Biblical Interpretation* (Grand Rapids: Wm. B. Eerdmans Publishing Co., 1950), p. 160.
[19]George Eldon Ladd, *Crucial Questions About the Kingdom of God* (Grand Rapids: Wm. B. Eerdmans Publishing Co., 1952), p. 138.

of interpretation, covenant theology produces artificial exegesis. This is the verdict of nondispensationalists against covenant theology. Listen to the church historian George Fisher:

> Cocceius carried the method of typical interpretation through the writings and the ceremonial institutions of the Old Testament. The exegesis in its particulars was often fanciful. Although he failed to apprehend the progressive character of Biblical revelation in this respect, that he made a system of grace pervade the Old Testament as it pervades the New, he yet made a fruitful beginning of Biblical theology.[20]

Orr assesses the results of the hermeneutics of covenant theology this way:

> . . . it failed to seize the true idea of development, and by an artificial system of typology, and allegorising interpretation, sought to read back practically the whole of the New Testament into the Old. But its most obvious defect was that, in using the idea of the Covenant as an exhaustive category, and attempting to force into it the whole material of theology, it created an artificial scheme which could only repel minds of simple and natural notions. It is impossible, e.g., to justify by Scriptural proof the detailed elaboration of the idea of a covenant of works in Eden, with its parties, conditions, promises, threatenings, sacraments, etc. Thus also the Reformed theology—the more that it had assumed this stiff and artificial shape—failed to satisfy the advancing intellect of the age. . . .[21]

This is a severe criticism from one who has no ax to grind for dispensationalism but who is looking at covenant theology from an historian's perspective. Notice that Orr charges covenant theology with (1) forced interpretation, (2) artifi-

[20]George Fisher, *History of Christian Doctrine* (Edinburgh: Clark, 1896), p. 349.
[21]Orr, *op. cit.*, pp. 303-4.

ciality, especially in typology, (3) no Biblical proof for the covenant of works, (4) failure to satisfy its age. These are the results of covenant theology's hermeneutics.

TWO WAYS OF SALVATION

We have pointed out how dispensationalists are charged with teaching two or more ways of salvation. One would think that this charge could never be leveled against covenant theology since its covenant of grace supposedly governs the way of salvation from Genesis 3:15 to the end of the Bible. Indeed, this pouring of the grace of God into a straitjacket is, according to the dispensationalist, the weakness of the covenant position. But what does the covenant theologian do with the matter of salvation under the law? Berkhof declares that "grace offers escape from the law only as a condition of salvation—as it is in the covenant of works—from the curse of the law . . ." and in another place he says, "From the law . . . both as a means of obtaining eternal life and as a condemning power believers are set free in Christ."[22] Allis declares positively, "The law is a declaration of the will of God for man's salvation."[23] Even Payne, a covenant premillennialist, for all his effort to keep from indicating that salvation during the period of the Law was by any means other than God's forgiveness in anticipation of the work of Christ, slips at one point and says:

> From the Mosaic period and onward, nonpresumptuous sins (Lev. 5:3) were specifically forgiven via the ritual law (v. 10; cf. Ps. 19:13) ; and other intentional violations were included as well (cf. Lev. 5:1, 4).[24]

These are very odd statements to find in the writings of covenant theologians if, as they say, "salvation has always

[22]Berkhof, *Systematic Theology*, pp. 291, 614.
[23]Oswald T. Allis, *Prophecy and the Church* (Philadelphia: Presbyterian and Reformed Publishing Co., 1945), p. 39.
[24]Payne, *op. cit.*, p. 414.

been one and the same; having the same promise, the same Saviour, the same condition, the same salvation."[25] Indeed, the law was a declaration of the will of God for man's salvation, and if sins could be forgiven via the ritual law, then covenant theology must be teaching two ways of salvation— one by law and one by grace! Covenant theology seems to teach the very "heresy" it accuses dispensationalism of teaching!

We have discovered some very interesting facts about covenant theology.

(1) Its origin was recent. It was not the doctrinal system of the ancient church. It did not originate with the Reformers, and actually its present form is a modification of the original covenant idea proposed by Cocceius and the Westminster Confession.

(2) The theological covenants on which covenant theology is based are not specifically revealed in Scripture. Other covenants are specifically revealed and in great detail, but these all-embracing covenants of covenant theology are not in the Bible. The whole covenant system is based on a deduction and not upon the results of an inductive study of Scripture.

(3) The hermeneutical straitjacket which covenant theology forces on the Scriptures results in reading the New Testament back into the Old and in an artificial typological interpretation. We discovered that this was the verdict of those who were not dispensationalists.

(4) For all its efforts to maintain a unity in the means of salvation, even covenant theology occasionally speaks about salvation by the Mosaic law. Does this mean that covenant theology teaches two ways of salvation?

The point of the chapter is simply this: The things which

[25]Charles Hodge, *Systematic Theology* (Wm. B. Eerdmans Publishing Co., 1946), II, 368.

are charged against dispensationalism can be charged with equal justice against covenant theology. How important these charges are is another question, and in stating them there is no implication about their importance. But the validity of the charges has been established, and if it is relevant to bring these accusations against dispensationalism, then it is equally relevant to bring the same charges against covenant theology. If these matters are not relevant to covenant theology, then covenant writers would do well to stop trying to make so much of them in their attacks on dispensationalism.

10

ULTRADISPENSATIONALISM

DISPENSATIONALISM and ultradispensationalism are related in some ways, but there are some very basic differences between the two schools of thought. The primary one is the difference over when the Church, the Body of Christ, began historically. Dispensationalists say that the Church began at Pentecost, while ultradispensationalists believe that it began sometime later. Both groups, however, recognize the clear distinction between Israel and the Church, and both interpret the Bible literally. Nevertheless, this difference over the beginning of the Church carries with it a number of other divergencies of teaching between the two groups. It affects the important matter of the ordinances, the relevance of the epistles, and the interpretation of the Gospels.

There are at least two reasons why a chapter on ultradispensationalism must be included in this book. First, it is necessary to distinguish the mainstream of dispensationalism from ultradispensationalism. Second, the charge that ultradispensationalism is only dispensationalism carried to its logical conclusion must be answered.

The prefix *ultra* is not a very accurate one when used as a theological label. It only means more extreme than the viewpoint held by the one who calls the other man ultra! People who hold views all the way from mild Arminianism to thoroughgoing Calvinism have been called ultra-Calvinists.

Some who are antidispensational label as ultradispensational what has been set forth as dispensationalism in this book. Anybody who divides Biblical history into various dispensational periods is in their judgment ultradispensational.[1] This is either a confusion due to misapprehension or a deliberate attempt to ridicule by the use of the ultra label. It is usually a successful tactic in these days, for we tend to shy away from anything that is ultra and not in the mainstream of thought or life.

Others insist that ultradispensationalism is only dispensationalism carried to its logical extremes. For instance, Allis declares:

> But Bullinger carried this method to such an extreme, a logical extreme we believe, that his teachings have been roundly denounced by what we may call the Scofield party; and Bullingerism has been stigmatized as "ultra" Dispensationalism.[2]

Fuller follows the same line.[3]

For these two reasons, then, it is necessary to give some consideration to the subject of ultradispensationalism.

THE ORIGIN OF ULTRADISPENSATIONALISM

Ultradispensationalism had its origin in the ministry and writings of Ethelbert W. Bullinger (1837-1913). He received his education at King's College, London, and was an ordained Anglican clergyman. He was the author of seventy-seven works, including the *Critical Lexicon and Concordance to the Greek New Testament* and the *Companion Bible*. He was a scholar of repute, editor for nineteen years of a monthly

[1]T. A. Hegre, *The Cross and Sanctification* (Minneapolis: Bethany Fellowship, 1960), p. 3.
[2]Oswald T. Allis, *Prophecy and the Church* (Philadelphia: Presbyterian and Reformed Publishing Co., 1945), p. 15.
[3]Daniel P. Fuller, "The Hermeneutics of Dispensationalism" (Doctor's dissertation, Northern Baptist Theological Seminary, Chicago, 1957), pp. 201-3.

magazine called *Things to Come,* and an accomplished musician.

His theology was a mixture. He held the heretical doctrine of the extinction of the soul between death and resurrection.[4] He was silent on the final state of the lost, and many of his followers were and are annihilationists. In his sevenfold dispensational scheme Bullinger had two dispensations between Pentecost and the end of the Church age. He placed the Gospels and the book of Acts under the law and commenced the dispensation of the Church with the ministry of Paul after Acts 28:28. The prison epistles, therefore—Ephesians, Philippians, and Colossians—set forth the fullness of the revelation of the mystery of this Church age. He also denied that water baptism and the Lord's Supper are for this age.

His dispensational teaching has been the fount of all the ultradispensational extremes from his day to the present. Not all, however, have followed all his extremes, but all, whether of the extreme or of the moderate group, hold tenaciously to the doctrine that the Church did not begin at Pentecost but did begin with Paul.

THE TYPES OF ULTRADISPENSATIONALISM

A. THE EXTREME TYPE

In England, the extreme dispensationalism of Bullinger was promulgated by his successor, Charles H. Welch of London. He divided the book of Acts into three sections: (1) restoration, the period when the kingdom was reoffered to Israel in Acts 1—9; (2) reconciliation, the period of Jew and Gentile; and (3) rejection of the nation Israel, which was not actually fulfilled until Acts 28 when Israel was set aside. Such division is typical of this school of dispensationalism.

In America, the extreme type was promoted by A. E. Knoch

---

[4]Ethelbert W. Bullinger, *The Rich Man and Lazarus or "The Intermediate State"* (London: Eyrie and Spottiswood, 1902).

and Vladimir M. Gelesnoff. Knoch is best known for his *Concordant Version of the Sacred Scriptures* published in Los Angeles in 1926 and completely revised in 1930. Knoch was even more extreme than Bullinger, seeing four dispensations from Christ to Paul's prison ministry. His followers included a number of extremists who boldly advocated annihilation and universal reconciliation. Less radical and more true to the original position of Bullinger was Otis Q. Sellers of Grand Rapids, Michigan. He followed Welch largely in his view of Acts.

B. The Moderate Type

The most widely known and influential ultradispensationalists in America are those associated with the Worldwide Grace Testimony (now known as Grace Mission), Grace Gospel Fellowship and the Berean Bible Society. Cornelius R. Stam, J. C. O'Hair, and Charles F. Baker are perhaps the best-known names connected with these groups. *Berean Searchlight* and *Truth* are representative magazines, and Grace Bible College in Grand Rapids, Michigan (formerly Milwaukee Bible Institute) teaches their point of view. A number of pamphlets and other writings have come from the pens of men in the movement.

As to doctrine, this group is agreed that the Church, the Body of Christ, began with Paul and did not begin on the day of Pentecost as recorded in Acts 2; however, they are not of one mind as to when the Church did actually begin. O'Hair placed its beginning at Acts 13, while Stam thought it began as early as Acts 9. Because they begin the Church before Acts 28 (in contrast to the extremist school) they do observe the Lord's Supper, but do not believe water baptism is for this Church age. In other words, they are sure when the Church did not begin, but not sure when it did begin!

C. COMPARISON OF THE TWO TYPES

POINTS OF AGREEMENT:

1. The great commission of Matthew and Mark is Jewish and not for the Church.
2. The ministry of the Twelve was a continuation of Christ's ministry.
3. The Church did not begin at Pentecost.
4. Water baptism is not for this Church age.
5. There is a difference between Paul's early and later ministries.
6. Israel, not the Church, is the Bride of Christ.

POINTS OF DIFFERENCE:

1. When did the Church begin? (Extreme—Acts 28. Moderate—before Acts 28.)
2. How long is the transition period in the book of Acts? (Extreme—until Acts 28. Moderate—until Acts 9 or13.)
3. What is the proper place of the Lord's Supper? (Extreme—no place. Moderate—proper to observe in the church.)
4. What Scripture is written to the Church primarily? (Extreme—Prison epistles only. Moderate—other Pauline epistles also.)

THE DEFINITION OF ULTRADISPENSATIONALISM

When one boils down the points of agreement and differences between the extreme and moderate schools of ultradispensationalists, he finds one outstanding difference remaining between ultradispensationalism and dispensationalism. It concerns the beginning of the Church, the Body of Christ. All ultradispensationalists, of whatever school, agree that it did not begin at Pentecost. All dispensationalists agree that it did. Therefore, ultradispensationalism may be defined, or certainly characterized rather definitively, as the school of interpretation which places more than one dispensation between Pentecost and the end of the Church age.

THE BEGINNING OF THE CHURCH IN ULTRADISPENSATIONALISM

As has been stated, the ultradispensationalists are certain that the Church did not begin at Pentecost although they are not sure among themselves when it did begin. The extreme group, which follows Bullinger, think that it began with the revelation of the mystery of the body of Christ to Paul during his first confinement in Rome; that is, it began near or after the close of the record of the book of Acts. As a result, the ordinances are not valid for this age since they are not mentioned in the epistles written from that Roman imprisonment. The moderate group holds that the Church began sometime before Paul wrote his first epistle, but exactly when is debated among those who hold this position. O'Hair evidently believed that the Church began with the pronouncement recorded in Acts 13:46: "We turn to the Gentiles," since after this event "there is no record that Paul or Peter, or any other messenger of the Lord, had divine authority to offer the prophesied kingdom to Israel, if that nation would repent."[5] Stam holds that the Church began before Acts 13, for to a degree the mystery was revealed to Paul at his conversion. "His conversion marked the *beginning* of the new dispensation."[6] In other words, the Church began in Acts 9. This is based on the fact that early in the book of Acts God was dealing with Jews and Peter was the chief spokesman. The Church, they say, could not have begun until God was dealing with Gentiles and primarily through Paul. To be very accurate, one should say that the ultradispensationalist be-

[5]J. C. O'Hair, *Important Facts to Understand Acts* (Chicago: O'Hair, n. d.), p. 22.
[6]Cornelius R. Stam, *Acts Dispensationally Considered* (Chicago: Berean Bible Society, 1954), II, 17.

lieves that the Body Church did not begin until after Paul came on the scene. The Jewish Church did begin at Pentecost, but this is different from the Church, the Body of Christ.

The interpretation of the book of Acts, the relation of the Gospels, the ordinances, the offer of the kingdom are all corollary subjects of the ultradispensationalists' doctrine of the beginning of the Church. While they are germane to the full development of ultradispensationalism, they are not relevant to the purpose of this chapter and reluctantly must be omitted.

ERRORS OF ULTRADISPENSATIONALISM

Dispensationalists believe that there are some very basic errors in the ultradispensational system and therefore they reject the system as diverse from their own and reject any implication that the two are similar.

A. Erroneous Concept of a Dispensation

In this book a dispensation has been defined as a distinguishable economy in the outworking of God's purpose. In relation to ultradispensationalism the definition raises this most pertinent question: Is something distinguishably different being done since Paul came on the scene that was not being done from Pentecost to the time of Paul? (It matters little to the answer to this question whether "Paul's coming on the scene" means Acts 9, 13, or 28.) Were there features and characteristics and doctrine of the Body Church before Paul? What the ultradispensationalist fails to recognize is that the distinguishableness of a dispensation is related to what God is doing, not necessarily to what He reveals at the time and least of all to what man understands of His purposes. It is certainly true that within the scope of any dispensation there is progressive revelation, and in the present one it is obvious that not all of what God was going to do was revealed on the day of Pentecost. These are economies of God, not of man, and we determine the limits of a dispensation not by what any one person within that dispensation understood but by what we may understand now from the complete revelation of the Word. Actually, we are in a better position to understand than the writers of the New Testament themselves.

Ultradispensationalists fail to recognize the difference between the progress of doctrine as it was during the time of revelation and the representation of it in the writing of the Scripture. On this point Bernard has well observed:

> . . . there would be a difference between the actual course of some important enterprise—say of a military campaign, for instance—and the abbreviated narrative, the selected documents, and the well-considered arrangement, by which its conductor might make the plan and execution of it clear to others. In such a case the man who read would have a more perfect understanding of the mind of the actor and the author than the man who saw; he would have the whole course of things mapped out for him on the true principles of order.[7]

The distinguishable feature of this economy is the formation of the Church which is Christ's Body. This is the work of God; therefore, the question which decides the beginning of this dispensation is, When did God begin to do this? not, When did man understand it? Only by consulting the completed revelation can we understand that God began to do this work on the day of Pentecost (Acts 1:5; 11:15-16; I Cor. 12:13; Col. 1:18), and therefore whether Peter and the others understood it then does not determine the beginning of the dispensation. The distinguishable feature of the present dispensation is the formation of the Church, and since the Church began at Pentecost there has been only one economy from Pentecost to the present. The ultradispensationalist can

[7]Thomas Dehany Bernard, *The Progress of Doctrine in the New Testament* (Grand Rapids: Zondervan Publishing House, n. d.), p. 35.

only offer the distinguishing feature of a Jewish Church as over against a Gentile Church which is the Body of Christ, but such a distinction has no validity because there are Jews in today's Gentile Church (even if it did not begin until after Pentecost) and because the baptism of the Spirit occurred in Jerusalem at Pentecost. Thus the same economy has been operative since the day of Pentecost.

B. Erroneous Exegesis of Key Passages

1. Passages concerning the Church. Whatever Church is mentioned before Paul is said by the ultradispensationalist to be the Jewish Church and not the Body Church. This forces an artificial and unnatural interpretation of some very basic passages. Paul stated that before his conversion he persecuted the Church of God (Gal. 1:13; 1 Cor. 15:9; Phil. 3:6). The natural understanding of these three references to the Church which Paul persecuted is that it was the same Church to which he and the converts won through his preaching were joined.

Furthermore, the first mention of the word *Church* in the book of Acts is explained as being "added to the Lord" (Acts 5:11, 14). This is no Jewish Church that is described in terms of its members being added to the Lord. As Ironside said in commenting on this verse: "This was before Paul's conversion. Observe it does not simply say that they were added to the company of believers, nor even to the assembly alone, but they were added to the Lord. This is only by a baptism of the Holy Spirit."[8] The converts in Antioch were also said to have been "added unto the Lord" (Acts 11:24). It is significant to note that Stam has no comment on this phrase. He bases his argument that this Church in Acts 5 was a Jewish one and not the Body Church on the fact that they were gathered in Solomon's porch![9] Such forced exegesis of these

[8]H. A. Ironside, *Wrongly Dividing the Word of Truth* (New York: Loizeaux Brothers), p. 33.
[9]Stam, *op. cit.*, I, 184.

passages using and explaining the word Church *before* Paul came on the scene is erroneous exegesis.

2. Ephesians 3:1-12. Ultradispensationalists are very fond of using this passage to attempt to prove that to Paul exclusively was revealed the mystery of the Church, the Body of Christ. If this is provable, then the mystery Church, the Body, could not have begun until Paul came on the scene. The most pointed critique of their use of this passage has been written (though unfortunately buried in a footnote) by dispensationalist Sauer. He says:

> In Eph. 3:3, Paul does not assert that he was the first to whom the mystery of the church had been made known. He says only that the secret counsel that there is no difference in the church between Jew and Gentile, and the equal rights of believing Gentiles and believing Jews had not been made known in the time (not before him personally but in general) before his generation, as it had now been revealed to "the holy apostles and prophets through the Spirit." The plural "apostles and prophets" is to be noted as implying that the revelation was not to Paul alone, and it was made to them "through the Spirit," not first by the agency of Paul (ver. 5). The "*as* it has *now* been revealed" may indeed suggest that this mystery had been hinted at in the Old Testament, but under veiled forms or types, and only now was properly revealed.
>
> What Paul does declare is that he had received this mystery by "revelation" (ver. 3). But he says no word as to the sequence of these Divine revelations or the question of priority of reception. The emphasis of ver. 3 does not lie on "me" but on "revelation." He does not use here the emphatic Greek *emoi*, but the unemphatic *moi*, and he places it (in the original text), not at the head of the sentence, but appends it as unaccented. On the contrary, to stress the word "revelation" he places it early in the sentence: "according to revelation was made

known to me the mystery." Here (as in Gal. 1:12) he
does not wish to declare any priority of time for himself
or that the revelation was given to him exclusively, but
only that he stood alone in the matter independently of
man. Not till Eph. 3:8, does he use the emphatic *emoi*
and place it at the head of the sentence. But there he is
not dealing with the first *reception* of the mystery but
with his *proclamation* of it among the nations. This, of
course, was then in fact the special task of Paul. He
was the chief herald of the gospel to the peoples of the
world.

[If one says: "I received this information from Mr.
Jones himself," this does not assert that Mr. Jones had
not formerly mentioned the matter to others. Trans.][10]

C. Other Passages Concerning the Revelation of the Mystery

The extreme type of ultradispensationalism is easily refuted
by several passages in which Paul says that he had been preaching the mystery long before the Roman confinement. In
Romans 16:25-27 he makes the plain statement that throughout the years his preaching had been in accordance with the
revelation of the mystery. (Bullinger said that these verses
were added to the epistle after he reached Rome several
years later!) First Corinthians 12 is a detailed revelation of
the mystery of the relationships of the Body of Christ. The
epistle was written before the Roman imprisonment. The
mystery of the Body Church was clearly revealed, known, and
proclaimed before Acts 28.

Arguments like these have forced many ultradispensationalists into the school of the moderates. However, certain
other considerations make it clear that Paul was not the first
or only one to speak of the mystery. The Lord said: "Other
sheep I have, which are not of this fold: them also I must

[10]Erich Sauer, *The Triumph of the Crucified* (Grand Rapids: Wm. B.
Eerdmans Publishing Co., 1952), p. 73n.

bring, and they shall hear my voice; and there shall be one flock, and one shepherd" (John 10:16). Furthermore, in the upper room just before His crucifixion He revealed the two basic mysteries of this Church age. He told His disciples (Paul was not one of them) : "At that day ye shall know that I am in my Father, and ye in me, and I in you" (John 14:20). The "ye in me" relationship is that of being in the Body of Christ of which He is the Head. The "I in you" relationship is that of His indwelling presence (Col. 1:27). The Body Church relationship was thus revealed by the Lord before His death, and it would be operative "at that day"; i.e., at the day when the Holy Spirit would come to be "in" them (John 14:17). When did this happen? It occurred on the day of Pentecost. On the day of Pentecost, then, they were placed in Him, and the Body Church began. That they may not have understood it we do not question, but the dispensation began when God began to do His distinguishably different work, not when or if ever man understood it.

D. BAPTISM "IN" THE SPIRIT

Before His ascension the Lord promised the disciples that they would be baptized *en pneumati* (Acts 1:5). In I Corinthians 12:13 Paul explains that being placed in the Body of Christ is accomplished by being baptized *en pneumati*. Since the promise of Acts 1:5 was fulfilled on the day of Pentecost (Acts 11:15-16), and if this is the baptism explained in I Corinthians 12:13 as effecting entrance into the Body of Christ, this is an irrefutable argument for the Body Church's beginning on the day of Pentecost. The ultradispensationalist realizes the strength of this argument, and he is forced to argue for two baptisms. Acts 1:5, he says, is a baptism "with" the Spirit for miraculous power and "this baptism with the Holy Spirit was not, of course, the baptism of Jews and Gentiles into one body."[11] The baptism of I Corinthians 12:13 is "by" the Spirit and this is the one that forms the Body Church.

Such a distinction is quite admissible as far as possible meanings of the same preposition *en* are concerned. The preposition does sometimes mean "with," "in" and "by." This is not contested. What is contested is the artificiality of making it mean one thing in Acts and another in I Corinthians *when it is used in exactly the same phrase with the word "Spirit."* For the sake of argument, let the ultradispensationalist face the possibility that in both instances it does mean the same and refers to the same baptism. Then his entire effort to make a separate dispensation of the early chapters of Acts of an alleged Jewish Church crashes to the ground. It makes little difference how the *en* is translated just as long as it is translated consistently in the verses which refer to baptism. Both the ASV and the RSV do this. The only normal way to understand these references to baptism *en pneumati* leads to the inescapable conclusion that the Body of Christ began at Pentecost and that there was no separate dispensation of a Jewish Church from Pentecost to the time of Paul.

These errors—in basic concept of a dispensation, in exegesis of key passages, in understanding when the mystery was revealed, in the baptizing work of the Spirit—are the reasons dispensationalists reject ultradispensationalism. The argument has been based not on the history or practice of the ultradispensational movement but strictly on Biblical evidence, for this is the evidence on which any school of thought ought to be judged. And on this basis ultradispensationalism is rejected.

It should be clear, too, that on the basis of the evidence presented, dispensationalism and ultradispensationalism have

[11]Stam, *op. cit.*, I, 30.

very basic differences. While it is true that antidispensationalists can level similar charges against both groups, this does not make the teaching of both groups the same. After all, one can level similar charges against liberals and Barthians, but this hardly makes liberalism and neoorthodoxy similar doctrinal systems. The same is true of dispensationalism and ultradispensationalism.

11

A PLEA

THIS BOOK HAS BEEN WRITTEN for two reasons: to try to correct some misconceptions about dispensationalism which have given rise to false charges against it, and to give a positive presentation of the system as it is being taught in the *latter* part of the twentieth century.

It is hoped that friends of dispensationalism will find it helpful to their own thinking. Certainly they will not be expected to agree with all the details presented. Those who are nondispensational or antidispensational will have to recognize at least that this is the dispensationalism being taught today (though the author in no way claims to speak for all contemporary dispensationalists) , and they should bring their thinking, writing, and even their attacks up to date.

However, this book would not be complete without a plea for integrity.

Every Christian has a right to his convictions about Biblical truth, but as long as we are in earthly bodies, none of us can be infallible. No one in any age has all the truth—not the apostolic fathers, nor the Reformers, nor dispensationalists, nor nondispensationalists. Nevertheless, we should hold with conviction the truth as we believe God has given us the understanding of it. False humility (which is often manifest these days in "broad-mindedness" and "rethinking") does not evince due credit to the teaching ministry of the Holy Spirit.

A cocksure attitude, on the other hand, does not give credence to the limitations and fallibility of the human mind. The balance between these extremes is well expressed in Paul's words: "Speaking the truth in love" (Eph. 4:15).

Both the dispensationalist and the nondispensationalist have a right to feel that their understanding of the Bible is the true one, but neither has the right to think or act as if he were the sole possessor of truth. And certainly both have a right to expect to have their views represented fairly and with integrity. Nothing is gained for one's viewpoint by running down the opposition.

Unfortunately, the representation of the dispensational viewpoint has not always been with integrity. For instance, chapter 6 points out how unfairly the dispensationalists' teaching on the matter of salvation is represented. Neither the older nor the newer dispensationalists teach two ways of salvation, and it is not fair to attempt to make them so teach. After all, a man has to be taken at his word or all means of communication break down. It is certainly fair to attempt to prove a position illogical, but it is never fair to misrepresent that position in the attempt. Straw men are easy to create, but the huff and puff it takes to demolish them are only huff and puff.

Dispensationalists have said enough about the Sermon on the Mount over a long period of time to make completely inappropriate such a statement as this from a recent writer, who is a man of great esteem and respect:

> That is the [dispensational] teaching: it says, in effect, that the Sermon on the Mount has nothing to do with us. . . . It is the law . . . of the kingdom of heaven, and has nothing whatsoever to do with Christians in the meantime.[1]

[1]D. Martyn Lloyd-Jones, *Studies in the Sermon on the Mount* (Grand Rapids: Wm. B. Eerdmans Publishing Co., 1959), I, 14-15.

This simply is not true. Dispensationalists do not teach that the Sermon has "nothing whatsoever to do with Christians in the meantime." To represent them as so saying does not evince integrity. Other examples have been mentioned elsewhere.[2]

As pointed out in the first chapter, another method of attack is to associate dispensationalists with higher critics, or liberals, or to list the dispensational interpretation of a doctrine along with the neoorthodox or liberal. All of this is the guilt-by-association method and is entirely unworthy of any conservative who uses it. After all, dispensationalism is a legitimate and conservative viewpoint. Another Christian does not have to agree with it, but he should represent it fairly. This is simply a matter of Christian integrity.

Integrity and a sense of priority go together. The temptation for any Christian preacher or writer to get off on a tangent or to ride a hobby is a very great one. This is true in doctrine, and it is true in matters of living. The age of specialization has caught up with the ministry so that some have lost their perspective of the whole and their sense of priority. The whole counsel of God is far more than the dispensational issue.

We all need priorities in our evaluation of doctrine. Some doctrines in the Bible are simply more important than others. Paul placed a high priority on the right understanding of the gospel (Gal. 1:8-9). He placed a low priority on the doctrine of the observance of particular days (Col. 2:16-17). Some doctrines should be given priority over others.

We who are dispensationalists would do well to remember this. "Dispensational truth" is not necessarily the most important thing in the Bible. Even prophecy, though a major

[2]Ronald Nash's strange statement about dispensationalists' alleged concern for incorporating the identity of the 144,000 in our church creeds; E. J. Carnell's attack on fundamentalists in his *Case* book; and the false charge about dispensationalists' supposed minimizing of the cross.

theme, should not constitute the whole of one's preaching. Victorious living, which is without question a high priority doctrine, can be overdone. This does not mean that a man should not be an expert or delve deeply in a certain area of truth, but it would not be inappropriate to ask God to give more experts in the whole counsel of God.

Of course, God gives gifts to the Church as He wills. But nowhere in the Bible do we read that the gift of teaching is restricted to teaching dispensationalism or prophecy or Christian living. The only restriction on the content of one's ministry is involved in the gift of evangelism which does limit the message of the evangelist to the gospel. Neither do we read anywhere in the Bible that the gift of helps or the gift of showing mercy is only to be exercised on those who believe strictly as we do. The gifts are to the body and the body is composed of dispensationalists and nondispensationalists!

Too, we need to be realistic about the matter of priority in fellowship. Fellowship means sharing in common, and all areas of fellowship are not equal simply because they do not involve the same sharing. Fellowship on the horizontal plane (that is, with other human beings) is like a series of concentric circles. The largest circle includes all men with whom we have a certain kind of fellowship. We are to do good to all men (Gal. 6:10) and to show respect in our speech to all men simply because all were created in the image of God (James 3:9). The next largest circle includes all Christians. We have a certain kind of fellowship with them regardless of their affiliations or beliefs. God has done something very wonderful and basic for every person in that circle of fellowship, and we share that in common. Some of the smaller circles may be our particular church fellowship or a doctrinal fellowship such as the writer personally shares in the seminary in which he teaches. Cutting across all these circles is the physical factor. We obviously do not share in the same measure in all circles the fellowship which we have within a given circle. Our Lord shared certain things with Peter, James, and John that He did not share with the others who were in that circle of the Twelve. As well as the physical factor, there may be legitimate sociological factors which cut across the circles.

The point is simply this: circles of fellowship are not in themselves wrong; it is our failure or refusal to recognize some of them that is wrong. When someone fails to recognize the larger circles and builds a wall of doctrine or practice around the smaller one, refusing to move out of these circles, he is in error. Equally wrong is the attempt to make believers have the same kind of fellowship with all other believers and not allow them to have the smaller circles of fellowship. It is obvious, too, that one's circles of responsibility follow closely the circles of fellowship.

Integrity exercised in all our varying relationships will do much toward cultivating a proper harmony among conservatives who may differ on the dispensational issue. It may seem strange that a book which supports such a sharply debated matter as dispensationalism should close with an appeal for harmony. It is hoped that this point will be read as carefully as the points of disagreement will be! It would be wishful thinking to expect every reader of this book to become a convinced dispensationalist, but we sincerely hope that we may clear some of the fog, settle some of the dust, and clearly see wherein we do differ and wherein we agree.

It may help to be reminded of some of the important doctrines to which dispensationalists subscribe wholeheartedly. After all, dispensationalists are conservatives and affirm complete allegiance to the doctrines of verbal, plenary inspiration, the virgin birth and deity of Christ, the substitutionary atonement, eternal salvation by grace through faith, the importance of godly living and the ministry of the Holy Spirit, and hope for the future in the coming of Christ. Those who are divided from us in the matter of dispensationalism and/or premillennialism may remember the areas in which they are united with us. As already noted, some doctrines are more important than others, so it particularly behooves us not to cut off our fellowship from those who share similar views about these important doctrines. There are few enough these days who believe in the fundamentals of the faith, and to ignore those who have declared themselves on the side of the truth of God may deliberately or unconsciously place us in strange associations. There seems to be something wrong with our circles of fellowship, sense of priority or doctrine or unity when we see conservatives viewing fellow conservatives as the opposition party and then finding their theological friends among those who are teaching and promoting error. There is something wrong, too, with our conception of wisdom and scholarship when we discount the teaching ministry of the Spirit.

There are, then, these large areas of agreement with dispensationalists. Even on the fringe of the area of disagreement (that is, the area of dispensational teaching) there are some points of agreement. Whether nondispensationalists want to acknowledge it or not, dispensationalists do believe in the unity of the plan of salvation, the unity of God's redeemed people in all ages, the present aspect of the kingdom of God, the single basis of salvation, the spiritual seed of Abraham, and even the possible validity of the covenant of grace! Our differences with nondispensationalists lie in three areas: (1) we believe in the clear distinction between Israel and the Church; (2) we affirm that normal or plain interpretation of the Bible should be applied consistently to all its parts; and (3) we avow that the unifying principle of the Bible is the glory of God and that this is worked out in several ways— the program of redemption, the program for Israel, the punishment of the wicked, the plan for the angels, and the glory of God revealed through nature. We see all these programs as means of glorifying God, and we reject the charge that by distinguishing them (particularly God's program for Israel from His purpose for the Church) we have bifurcated God's purpose.[3] Actually, the Biblical revelation does more than bifurcate God's purpose (which means to divide in two) ; it divides it into at least five distinct purposes, all of which are united in the single purpose of glorifying God.

These are the basic distinctions of dispensationalism; and we believe them to be a help, not a heresy.

[3]Daniel P. Fuller, "The Hermeneutics of Dispensationalism" (Doctor's dissertation, Northern Baptist Theological Seminary, Chicago, 1957), pp. 371-72.

SELECTED BIBLIOGRAPHY

This selected list contains principal works for and against dispensationalism with brief annotations. The footnotes in the book cite additional works. Bibliographies of premillennial works can be found elsewhere (J. Dwight Pentecost, *Things to Come* [Findlay, Ohio: Dunham Publishing Co., 1958], and John F. Walvoord, *The Millennial Kingdom* [Findlay, Ohio: Dunham Publishing Co., 1959]). Standard works of theology are not included either.

Representative dispensational authors of former days include James H. Brookes, Lewis Sperry Chafer, John N. Darby, Arno C. Gaebelein, Harry A. Ironside, William Kelly, C. H. Mackintosh, and C. I. Scofield. More recent dispensationalists include E. Schuyler English, Charles L. Feinberg, Alva J. McClain, René Pache, J. Dwight Pentecost, Erich Sauer, and John F. Walvoord.

Ultradispensationalism is presented in the writings of Cornelius R. Stam. See his *Things That Differ* (Chicago: Berean Bible Society, 1959) and *Moses and Paul* (Chicago: Berean Bible Society, 1956).

In addition to the writings of these authors, the following books and articles are deemed particularly germane to this study of dispensationalism:

ALLIS, OSWALD T. *Prophecy and the Church.* Philadelphia: Presbyterian and Reformed Publishing Co., 1945. A classic attack on dispensational premillennialism by an amillennial scholar.

BASS, CLARENCE B. *Backgrounds to Dispensationalism.* Grand Rapids: Wm. B. Eerdmans Publishing Co., 1960. The thesis of this book is that dispensationalism is erroneous and dangerous because it is not the historic teaching of the Church and because it is divisive. The book is excellent on the life of J. N. Darby and contains a complete bibliography of Darby's works.

BOWMAN, JOHN WICK. "The Bible and Modern Religions: II. Dispensationalism," *Interpretation,* April, 1956, pp. 170-87. A diatribe against the Scofield Reference Bible.

CHAFER, LEWIS SPERRY. *Dispensationalism.* Dallas: Dallas Seminary Press, 1936. A brief statement of the relation of dispensationalism to various areas of doctrine by the founder of Dallas Theological Seminary.

———. *Systematic Theology.* 8 vols. Dallas: Dallas Seminary Press, 1947. A complete and standard systematic theology written from the dispensational and premillennial viewpoint.

EHLERT, ARNOLD H. "A Bibliography of Dispensationalism," *Bibliotheca Sacra,* 1944-1946. An exhaustive study of the history of dispensational interpretation.

FULLER, DANIEL PAYTON. "The Hermeneutics of Dispensationalism." Unpublished Th.D. dissertation, Northern Baptist Theological Seminary, Chicago, 1957. In this work the dean of Fuller Theological Seminary espouses the covenant premillennial view in opposition to dispensationalism.

IRONSIDE, H. A. *Wrongly Dividing the Word of Truth.* (3rd ed.) New York: Loizeaux Brothers, 1938. A brief refutation of ultradispensational teaching.

KRAUS, C. NORMAN. *Dispensationalism in America.* Richmond: John Knox Press, 1958. An attack on 1909 dispensationalism. The Mennonite author is as disturbed about dispensationalism's emphasis on such doctrines as inspiration and depravity as he is about the dispensational scheme itself.

LADD, GEORGE E. *Crucial Questions About the Kingdom of God.* Grand Rapids: Wm. B. Eerdmans Publishing Co., 1952.

———. *The Gospel of the Kingdom.* Grand Rapids: Wm. B. Eerdmans Publishing Co., 1959. A nondispensational but premillennial interpretation of key issues and passages.

LINCOLN, C. FRED. "The Development of the Covenant Theory," *Bibliotheca Sacra,* January, 1943. An important article on the history of covenant theology.

McCLAIN, ALVA J. *The Greatness of the Kingdom.* Grand Rapids: Zondervan Publishing House, 1959. A dispensational, premillennial eschatology by the former president of Grace Theological Seminary.

RHODES, ARNOLD B. (ed.). *The Church Faces the Isms.* New York: Abingdon Press, 1958. Essays by members of the faculty of the Louisville Presbyterian Theological Seminary. The chapter on dispensationalism exhibits an unfortunate attitude toward dispensationalism based upon limited research and emotional reactions to certain experiences.

SAUER, ERICH. *The Dawn of World Redemption.* Grand Rapids: Wm. B. Eerdmans Publishing Co., 1955.

———. *The Triumph of the Crucified.* Grand Rapids: Wm. B. Eerdmans Publishing Co., 1952. These two books are Old and New Testament Biblical theology at its finest by a German dispensationalist.

———. *From Eternity to Eternity.* London: Paternoster Press, 1954. The history of salvation unfolded in the progress of revelation. An excellent apologetic for dispensationalism.

SCOFIELD, C. I. (ed.). The Scofield Reference Bible. New York: Oxford University Press, 1909.

———. *Rightly Dividing the Word of Truth.* Various publishers. A simple and brief Bible study booklet highlighting dispensational doctrinal distinctives.

SUBJECT INDEX

Allis, O. T., 11, 35, 90, 98-99, 112, 133, 162, 166-67, 184
Apostasy, 150-54
Augustine, 69-70

Bass, C. B., 12, 13, 66, 78, 101-2, 110-11, 132, 162, 171-72
Berkhof, L., 15, 35, 43-44, 112-13, 119, 140-41, 178, 187
Bowman, J. W., 11, 12, 23, 27-28, 48-49, 110
Bullinger, E. W., 193-94

Calvin, John, 41, 67
Chafer, L. S., 16, 24, 45, 54, 113, 114, 120, 144, 163-64, 169, 183
Church
  and apostasy, 150-54
  and Israel, 44-45, 95-96, 137-40, 159
  and kingdom, 144-46
  and saints of other ages, 146-48
  and seed of Abraham, 148-50
  in covenant theology, 140-44
  in dispensationalism, 132-44
  in ultradispensationalism, 197-98
Cocceius, 180-82, 188
Conscience, dispensation of, 58-59
Covenant Theology, 18, 46, 50, 93
  definition of, 177-78
  church in, 140-44
  history of, 178-83
  salvation in, 112-13, 122-23
Cross, 161-68

Darby, J. N., 74-76, 78, 99, 156-57
Davidic covenant, 120-21, 166
Dispensation(s) and dispensationalism
  characteristics of, 36-39
  cross in, 161-68
  definition of, 29-33
  etymology of, 24-25
  history of, 67-78
  number of, 48-52
  sine qua non, 43-47

Fuller, D. P., 11, 28, 29, 40, 44-45, 48, 65, 93-95, 97, 99, 102, 111, 115-16, 124, 142, 212

Government, dispensation of, 59-60
Grace
  dispensation of, 62-63, 115
  relation to law, 117-19

Hermeneutics, 20, 45-46, 86-98, 158-59, 187-89
Holy Spirit
  baptism of, 136-37, 203-4
  in O. T., 120

Innocency, dispensation of, 57-58
Israel, see Church and Israel

Judgments, 39

Kingdom
  despiritualizing of, 168-69
  of God and of heaven, 170-74

Kraus, C. N., 42, 81, 105

Ladd, G. E., 20, 21, 46, 68, 91, 105, 107, 141-42, 161, 166, 170-71
Literal interpretation, see Hermeneutics

Millennium, 63-64, 75, 146-47, 160-61, 174-76
Mosaic dispensation, 53-54, 61-62, 115, 120-21, 146

Noahic dispensation, 52-53
Nondispensational premillennialism, 91, 96-97, 143, 160-61, 167

Philosophy of history, 16-20, 39-43
Philosophy of language, 87-88
Postponement of kingdom, 162-64
Premillennialism, 44

217

SCRIPTURE INDEX

Moody Press, a ministry of the Moody Bible Institute, is designed for education, evangelization and edification. If we may assist you in knowing more about Christ and the Christian life, please write us without obligation to: Moody Press, c/o MLM, Chicago, Illinois 60610.